MADE
Perfect
Weakness

MADE *Perfect* IN *Weakness*

Formerly titled, *How to Get It Right After You've Gotten It Wrong*

Gary J. Oliver

Chariot VICTOR
PUBLISHING
A DIVISION OF COOK COMMUNICATIONS

ChariotVictor Publishing, a division
of Cook Communications, Colorado Springs, Colorado 80918
Cook Communications, Paris, Ontario
Kingsway Communications, Eastbourne, England

Some people's names and certain details of case studies mentioned in this book
have been changed to protect the privacy of the individuals involved.

Editors: Larry Weeden, Greg Clouse

Design: Paul Higdon, Scott Rattray, Bill Gray

ISBN: 1-56476-719-1

Dedication

For my wife Carrie

Your fervent love for Jesus, your love for me and the boys, your faithful friendship, and your tenacious commitment to a great marriage are only a few of the attributes that make you precious to me. More than anyone else God has used you to help me learn how to get it right after I've gotten it wrong. I told you it might take some time. You are and always will be my one and only.

For my sons Nathan, Matthew, and Andrew

You have given me laughter and joy, you have taught me compassion, tenderness, and patience. You've taught me how to listen. Your love for me and your love for Jesus are priceless treasures. It is an honor and a privilege to be your dad.

Acknowledgments

This has been one of the most challenging books I've written. Throughout the process there were several individuals and couples whose encouragement, example, support, suggestions, and faithful prayers were invaluable. My sincere appreciation and thanks to:

Chip and Cheryl Carmichael, Doug and Joyce Feil, Bill Gaither, Monte Hasz, Steve and Twila Lee, Bill and Lyndi McCartney, George and Leona Oliver, Marsha Oliver, Randy and Holly Phillips, James and Belinda Ryle, Ed and Lanell Schilling, Dale and Liz Schlafer, Greg and Erin Smalley, Mark O. Sweeney, Jim and Barb Tallant, Warren Wiersbe, Norm and Joyce Wright, my friends at PromiseKeepers and Back to the Bible, as well as the dedicated staff of men and women at Southwest Counseling Associates that I have the privilege to work with.

And a special thanks to Larry K. Weeden, husband, father, humorist, men's small group advocate, encourager, and gifted editor whose commitment to excellence continues to be a source of inspiration.

Contents

1. Finding God in Our Failures

Don was one of my best friends in seminary. He loved the Lord, was a committed father and husband, and had a great sense of humor. We hit it off immediately. During our three years together, we studied, prayed, played, laughed, cried, camped, and fished together. I don't know if I could have gotten through Greek without his help. And Don's senior sermon on Romans 8:1-4 was one of the best.

After graduation, Don, his wife, Karen, and their family moved from Southern California to a little church in New Jersey. Before long, the church was growing. For the first few years after their move, we talked and corresponded several times a year. Over time, however, our communication dwindled to the annual Christmas card and a periodic phone call.

Last year, I didn't get a Christmas card from Don. It had been over a year since we had talked, so I tried to give him a call. I couldn't believe what I heard at the church office: Don was no longer the pastor there, the secretary said. By the tone of her voice, I could tell there was more to the story, so I looked up his home number.

Karen answered the phone. After the usual greetings, I asked to speak to Don, and she said, "Haven't you heard?"

"Heard what?" I asked.

She went on to tell me that eight months earlier, Don had resigned from the church, filed for divorce, and moved to Indiana. As I got the story from her and later from Don after tracking him down, it seems he had grown bored in the ministry. Then he got emotionally involved with the wife of one of his deacons, a relationship that started innocently but eventually became a full-blown affair. When Karen had sensed the growing distance between them, she had suggested they go for counseling, but Don's response had been, "Someone who knows the Bible as well as I do shouldn't need counseling."

How incredibly sad! What an unbelievable waste! A good man had chosen to throw away his wife, his children, his friends, his ministry, his reputation, and his faith. He hadn't just failed; he had become a failure.

Mimi learned at an early age that her parents' love was conditional, based on her performance. "When I was a little girl, I learned that anger was a forbidden emotion," she told me with a halting voice and misty eyes. Now a thirty-four-year-old mother of three, she continued, "Whenever I expressed anger as a child, my parents would emotionally withdraw from me. I remember feeling so alone and such a failure."

Not surprisingly, the lesson she learned was, "If I express anger, I won't be loved." So over time, she came to fear anger. And instead of learning how to use it to clarify and strengthen her own identity, she learned to do a great job of ignoring her anger. She became a people pleaser, adept at reading people and giving them what they wanted.

What brought Mimi to me for counseling was that she was finding it harder and harder to control her temper. "Things will go along great for several weeks, and then — sometimes over the tiniest provocation — I'll lose it," she told me. "At first, it would build gradually. But lately, all of a sudden I find myself shouting at my kids or lashing out at my husband."

Mimi had spent a lifetime burying her anger, and now, like an emotional Mount St. Helens, the pressure was getting too strong. It was erupting, and she was feeling guilty and ashamed. Because she had never learned to understand and control her anger, it was now controlling her.

Don and Mimi. Two different people. One's failure was due to unwise decisions and blatant sin. The other's was due to poor modeling and the power of bad habits. One faced an enormous failure, and the other had to deal with a series of small failures. But both felt discouraged, defeated, and helpless.

Like me, you've seen many examples of failure. You've heard many different words to describe it. You've experienced it yourself more times than you care to admit. But whatever the shape, size, sound, intensity, or color of the package, in some way it always involves the queasy and unsettling feeling of falling short. Of being inadequate. Of being not quite good enough.

It doesn't matter how many people know about it. It may have taken place in private, like Mimi's, or it might have been widely known, like Don's. It doesn't matter how many times it happens. You never like it. You never get used to it. You don't want it to happen again.

Nor does it matter how much you were able to control it. You might have had total control over it, or you might have had nothing to do with it. You might have been the sole cause or an innocent bystander.

It doesn't even matter how big or small it is. You might have almost made it, or perhaps you missed it by a mile and fell flat on your face. It may have put only a speck of dust on your perfect record, or it may have disqualified you from ministry. Nevertheless, the embarrassing, uncomfortable, and draining feeling is still there.

You can use any word you want to describe it. You can call it a blunder, error, *faux pas,* slip, setback, shellacking, trip, trouncing, thrashing, miss, muff, mistake, reversal, rebuff, rout, licking, lambasting, clobbering, comedown, loss, tragedy, drubbing, debacle, disappointment, or defeat. But the world around us and that little hard-to-ignore voice inside call it *failure.*

If I asked you to make a list of your top ten fears, what

would you include? Which fear would be at the top? I've had hundreds of people do this little exercise, and the majority of people, most of whom were Christians, consistently listed the fear of failure in the top five.

There are several components to this fear. First comes our fear of making a mistake. Closely related to that is the fear of someone finding out that we made a mistake. And that leads to what is, for some, the paralyzing fear of what will happen when others discover the mistake. They might make fun of us, think less of us, or even break off their relationship with us.

So what do we do? We do what men and women have done since the beginning of time. In Genesis we read that when Adam and Eve sinned, they hid from God and from each other. They tried to cover up their failure. It's inherent in fallen human nature to hide our flaws and failures or to hurl the blame for those mistakes on others. Some of us are good at both hiding and hurling. That's just what Adam and Eve did, and that's what we do. As Charlie Brown once said, "There is no problem so big that I can't run from it."

This response is not confined to those who aren't Christians. Think about it. If visitors from outer space paid an initial visit to a local evangelical church, they might go away thinking no one in that congregation ever made a mistake. In the weekly testimony service, we hear glowing reports of what God is doing in our lives. The weekly prayer meetings are filled with requests for the problems and mistakes of others, but rarely is there an acknowledgment of *my* mistake and a request for God to help *me* learn from it.

Now, don't misunderstand me. There's nothing wrong with wanting to succeed, to be the best we can be. God wants us to succeed. He delights in blessing His people. He wants to help us become more than conquerors.

The problem, however, is that many of us have gotten sucked into the world's definition of success. Some of us have moved beyond pursuing excellence to pursuing perfection. And our standard for measuring perfection is a total absence of flaws or failures. Our desire to be the best becomes the focal point of our lives. Our identity, worth, and security become based in our relentless pursuit of perfection. When this happens, enough is never enough. We're in the fast lane for failure.

Why is failure so feared? Why has it become the scarlet letter? Why do we invest so much time and energy denying our deficiencies and hiding our weaknesses? Where did we learn to fear failure?

Not only are we born with this flawed failure response, inherited from Adam and Eve, but it's also cultivated in us from an early age. Before we develop the ability to do complex abstract thinking, we learn in ways we don't know we're learning that success is good and failure is bad, and we learn how our parents and others define those terms.

In some homes like Mimi's, love is offered as a reward for successful behavior, and the withholding of love and affection becomes the punishment for failure. In these homes, we learn to equate love with perfection and rejection with failure. When we're successful in something like schoolwork or sports, we're encouraged, rewarded, and praised. This is often accompanied by a touch—a hug or a kiss. It's clear that we're valuable and loved. But when we fail, we're punished, humiliated, and perhaps even isolated. If we're touched, it's rarely a soft, gentle, comforting touch that communicates that our value doesn't depend on our performance.

Since failure is so painful and clearly unacceptable to our parents and teachers, we learn to develop strategies for denying, concealing, or distorting our failures while at the same time lauding, exaggerating, or even fabricating our victories.

When we leave school and enter the business and professional community, we discover that we're prepared to succeed in a community where it's equally unwise to admit any error or failure. However, at this level, the appearance of success becomes even more important. The stakes have been raised. Our self-respect, reputation, livelihood, and perhaps even our desire to live may be on the line.

Why Would Anyone Want to Read a Book about Failure?

I've wanted to write this book for years. But my sense that no one would want to pick up a book with the word *failure* in the title led me to other writing pursuits. However, God has refused to let me keep this in the back of my mind. He has continued to remind me of the need to help Christians look at failure through His eyes so they can understand what He can accomplish through it in their lives. *I want to show you in this book the amazing things God can do with failure.*

In 1967, in a small church in Anaheim, California, I started my first discipleship group. In meeting with those young Christians committed to growing in Christ, I came face-to-face with questions that I find myself and others still asking twenty-five years later.

An important part of discipleship involves understanding God's promises to us. One of the best ways to understand them is to memorize them. So part of this discipleship program involved memorizing one promise a week. Every time we met, we would quote the new promise and then repeat all those we had already learned. It was an encouraging and fruitful exercise. As those young Christians learned about God's promises, however, a few questions arose.

In John 10:10, for example, Jesus said, "I have come that they may have life, and have it to the full." In Ephesians 3:20, Paul described God as one who wants to do "exceeding abundantly beyond all that we ask or think" (NASB). In Philippians 4:13, Paul told us that we can do all things through Christ who gives us strength. Those are great promises, and they're all true.

But here's the rub. If Christ came for us to have an abundant life; if He wants that life to be exceedingly abundantly beyond all we ask or think; and if we can do all things through Him who strengthens us—then why do we experience such frequent failure? Why do we repeat the same mistakes over and over? Why do so many Christians spend years stuck in the same moral or behavioral ruts? Why are so many of us dominated by our fear of failure? Can we learn from our failures? If so, how? Is failure the opposite of maturity, or is it a part of the process of becoming mature?

For more than twenty-five years, I've worked with people stuck in their efforts to grow. They've wanted to be successful but have felt like lifelong failures. Some have kept on trying. Others have settled for a life of what feels like safety and security, but what results in mediocrity and stagnation. Not only have I worked with those people, at times I've even *been* one of those people.

For more than twenty-five years, people have walked into my office overwhelmed by the demands, discouragements, and difficulties of life. Many come for counseling only as a last resort. And after thousands of hours of talking with people, I made a phenomenal discovery. I had seen it for years, but it was so simple that I hadn't noticed it.

In most cases, the crisis that led people to call for the initial appointment was an experience that had happened to them many times before. But rather than identify the problem, understand it, and learn from it, they had tried to get through it as quickly as possible and, in many cases, pretend it never even happened. On a short-term basis, that strategy appeared to work well. Few people, if any, knew there had been a problem. Their reputation wasn't tarnished. Their ego wasn't damaged. And armed with a myopic optimism, they charged ahead to meet the next challenge.

Unfortunately, they charged ahead ill-prepared and ill-equipped. Why? Because the problem that had led to the first failure had never been admitted, addressed, defined, dissected, and learned from. So it was inevitable that in a matter of weeks, months, or in some cases years, it happened again. The only difference was that this time it was a bit larger, a bit more painful, and much more difficult to ignore.

Yet even with the increased pain, their response was the same — minimize, deny, ignore, explain away, and move on. What finally brought them in for counseling was that they could no longer ignore the problem. It had gotten so large and so painful that they had to deal with it. And that's what normally happens. Most people won't reach out for help until their pain becomes greater than their fear.

Most of us don't understand the value of failure. We don't realize that one of the best ways to avoid future failure is to face the present one when it occurs and learn from our mistakes — to allow God to meet us in our failures. How about you? How do you respond to failure? What have you learned from your mistakes?

This isn't really a book about failure as much as it's a book about the role of failure in the process of sanctification. It's a book about God's incredible love for us, His desire for us to grow and mature, and His provision of all we'll ever need to become conformed to our Lord Jesus Christ.

What Is Failure?

What do you think of when you hear the word *failure?* How would you define it? The word came into English from a Latin word meaning "to deceive or disappoint." The words *fallacy* and *fallible* derive from the same root. Failure can be defined as the condition of not achieving the desired end or ends; the condition of being found insufficient or falling short. When we fail, we have proved ourselves to be deficient, unsuccessful, or undependable; we've lost.

In many cases, failure involves a psychological crisis and its accompanying anguish and confusion. "Failure is not just the absence of success but a force in its own right. It is almost always painful, and in this respect it bears an unnerving resemblance to the painfulness of both death and birth. Indeed, failure is both death and birth, and it challenges us to embrace it as such."[1]

Failure can be something we do or something that happens to us. But it usually involves more than that. Failure is also an *interpretation* we make about what's happened. And that interpretation will determine how it affects our lives. As we'll see in a future chapter, this interpretation plays a critical role in determining how we grow. We can judge *our performance* in an event to have failed, or we can judge *ourselves* a failure. In this book, I'll be referring to failure in both ways.

The road to maturity is filled with many different potholes and detours. Just when we think we're on a roll, we've got it down pat, we've put our lives on cruise control . . . it happens. We hit what initially seems like an obstacle or barrier. We find ourselves on the wrong road and aren't sure how we got there.

But the amazing thing is that what initially seems to be a setback may be just the opposite. What apart from God feels like a failure can, in His skilled hands, become a part of His provision for our growth. We can't be successful in the Christian life if we deny the existence of failure. Anything that's painful or makes us feel unworthy — mistakes; setbacks; our own capacity for selfishness, anger, or cruelty; memories of injury or abuse at the hands of others — can be the fodder for failure or provide the raw materials for a stronger foundation. If we learn how to value it, understand it, and take it to the foot of the cross, we can become wiser and stronger because of it.

John Keats expressed it well when he said, "Failure is, in a sense, the highway to success, inasmuch as every discovery of what is false leads us to seek earnestly after what is true, and every fresh experience points out some form of error which we shall afterward carefully avoid."[2]

When God began to challenge my understanding of failure, my first question was, "What does the Bible have to say about this?" Well, I didn't have to go far to discover that God's Word has a lot to say about failure. From Genesis to Revelation, we find the record of repeated failures. I discovered that we all have a lot in common with Adam and Eve, the Children of Israel, David, Thomas, and Peter.

In fact, if you turn to Hebrews 11 and look at the "Hall of Faith," you'll find the names of Noah, Abraham, Sarah, Isaac, Jacob, Moses, and Rahab. Every one of them was a "loser" who became a "winner" because of what they learned from their failures. But before we can become winners, there are five facts about failure that we simply must understand.

Five Facts about Failure

1. Failure is inevitable

You can't have your mother write a note to get you excused from the school of hard knocks. An occupational hazard of being human is that we'll make mistakes, experience setbacks, fall short, and fail. Cadavers never fail; they're calm, cool, and laid back. But they never accomplish anything, either. For those of us who are conscious and attempt even the smallest task, there is always the probability that we'll experience failure.

It doesn't matter how old you are, how smart you are, or how spiritual you are. Look at the Apostle Paul. By the time he wrote the Book of Romans, he had made three prolonged missionary journeys. He had pioneered the Christian message throughout the eastern provinces of the Roman Empire. He had suffered persecution, made converts, discipled new believers, and established churches. What we're talking about here is not just someone who knew God's Word. The Holy Spirit used the Apostle Paul to *write* God's Word.

So here we have this godly, wise, mature giant of the faith. But when we read what he wrote in Romans 7, we discover that he still struggled, got stuck, and blew it. Look at verses 15 through 23.

I don't understand myself at all, for I really want to do what is right, but I can't. I do what I don't want to—what I hate. I know perfectly well that what I am doing is wrong, and my bad conscience proves that I agree with these laws I am breaking. But I can't help myself, because I'm no longer doing it. It is sin inside me that is stronger than I am that makes me do these evil things. I know I am rotten through and through so far as my old sinful nature is concerned. No matter which way I turn I can't make myself do right. I want to but I can't. When I want to do good, I don't; and when I try not to do wrong, I do it anyway. . . . It seems to be a fact of life that when I want to do what is right, I inevitably do what is wrong. I love to do God's will so far as my new nature is concerned; but there is something else deep within me, in my lower nature, that is at war with my mind and wins the fight and makes me a slave to the sin that is still within me. In my mind I want to be God's willing servant but instead I find myself still enslaved to sin (Rom. 7:15-19, 21-23, TLB).

Several years later we find an older, wiser, and even more mature Paul who wrote to the believers in Philippi:

I don't mean to say I am perfect. I haven't learned all I should even yet, but I keep working toward that day when I will finally be all that Christ saved me for and wants me to be. No, dear brothers, I am still not all I should be but I am bringing all my energies to bear on this one thing: Forgetting the past and looking forward to what lies ahead, I strain to reach the end of the race and receive the prize for which God is calling us up to heaven because of what Christ Jesus did for us (Phil. 3:12-14, TLB).

Let's not kid ourselves. As long as we have life and breath, we'll struggle with the consequences of our sinful humanity. The only real question is, will we go through life making the same mistakes, repeating the same failures, over and over? Or will we stop, look, listen, and learn? You see, failure really isn't that special. The best people fail frequently. Letting God teach you how to *learn* from failure is what's special and mature.

2. Failure reminds me that I am not God

Failure reveals the fact that we're ordinary, fallible, fallen people. And somewhere we've been tricked into believing that God can't use plain old, ordinary, fallible people. If we hope to be loved, valued, and happy, we have to be successful. In fact, we have to be perfect.

But that isn't what God's Word teaches us. In James 5:17, we read that the great Prophet Elijah "was a man just like us." In Acts 4:13, we read that the great apostles Peter and John were "ordinary" men. If you read the Book of Exodus, you'll find that Moses was also an extraordinarily ordinary man. Moses not only experienced failure, he even built his early ministry on it. In Exodus 3, when God first called him into leadership, his fear of failure sent him into a panic. Moses dredged up every weakness, focused on every flaw, thought up every excuse he could to disqualify himself. Finally he began to get the message that it wasn't about him. It was about the fact that God had chosen him.

When Moses did finally take his first baby steps toward maturity, his performance wasn't warmly received. He didn't get a standing ovation. His first attempts were responded to with rejection and sneers rather than success. He was still young. He still had a lot to learn.

His impulsivity, immaturity, and inability to handle his anger led to forty years in the wilderness. When I was younger, I viewed those as "wasted" years. But the Almighty God used that time to refine Moses and transform him into a strong leader. When Moses finally returned to Egypt from the obscurity of the wilderness, he was a changed man.

When Moses chose to learn from his mistakes, God was able to use him in mighty ways. But Moses also learned the high cost of not learning. From an early age, he had struggled with his anger. Remember, that's what had gotten him into trouble in the first place. While he gained some control over it, he never allowed God to help him master it. Eventually his inability to learn from his repeated failures cost him a trip into the Promised Land.

In Philippians 3:10, Paul expressed his desire to "know Christ and the power of His resurrection and the fellowship of sharing in His sufferings." It's easy for me to pray for the power of His resurrection, but I rarely ask to participate in the fellowship of His sufferings. Through the struggle and suffering that come from those big and little failures, however, we're reminded of who we are and who He is.

If you ever feel weak, powerless, discouraged, frustrated, limited . . . if you feel ordinary . . . you are prime material for God to use. Time and again, the Bible clearly tells us that our God *deliberately* seeks out the weak and the despised things, because it's from them that He can receive the greatest glory. In 1 Corinthians 1, Paul wrote:

> Notice among yourselves, dear brothers, that few of you who follow Christ have big names or power or wealth. Instead, God has deliberately chosen to use ideas the world considers foolish and of little worth in order to shame those people considered by the world as wise and great. He has chosen a plan despised by the world, counted as nothing at all, and used it to bring down to nothing those the world considers great, so that no one anywhere can ever brag in the presence of God (1 Cor. 1:26-29, TLB).

3. Failure helps me find God and see things through His eyes
Failure can be God's way of tapping us on the shoulder to get our attention. We can almost hear Him say, "Hello? Anyone home? Remember Me? Remember why I died and rose again?" Once we're reminded of our ordinariness, we're in a much better place to see His grace, His goodness, and His power. Look at the lives of Jonah, Moses, and David before and after their failures. They were different people. They weren't different because they failed, however, but because they learned from and grew through their failure.

In the darkness of defeat, it's easy to develop a fault focus rather than a faith focus. We dwell on what we *can't* do rather than on what He *can* do. When we fail, Satan wants us to divert our focus to dried-up streams so we don't see the rivers of living water that are always readily available. That's why failure often leads to a crisis of belief that requires a conscious decision to turn our focus from ourselves and our failures to Jesus.

God loves to build on our weaknesses, our mistakes, our failures. He takes the ruins of our brave (and at times vain) attempts and fashions the seemingly useless pieces of rubble into a life that brings Him praise and honor. Those aren't the building materials we would use. But our weak wills, inadequate resources, inconsistent efforts, and imperfect vision are being transformed by His power. Out of the wreck and ruin of our selfishness, sinfulness, and foolishness, He is making something beautiful. Bill and Gloria Gaither say it best:

"Something Beautiful"

If there ever were dreams that were lofty and noble,
They were my dreams at the start.
And the hopes for life's best were the hopes that I harbored
Down deep in my heart.
But my dreams turned to ashes, my castles all crumbled,
My fortune turned to loss,
So I wrapped it all in the rags of my life,
And laid it at the cross!
Something beautiful, something good;
All my confusion, He understood.
All I had to offer Him was brokenness and strife,
But He made something beautiful of my life.[3]

That's how our God works. He takes what we might consider foolish and ordinary and transforms it. The psalmist wrote, "As a father has compassion on his children, so the Lord has compassion on those who fear Him; for He knows how we are formed, He remembers that we are dust" (Ps. 103:13-14). It's true. We're nothing more than dust. But the Bible tells us that we are cherished and redeemed dust. We're dust that God has created to be "a little lower than the heavenly beings and crowned . . . with glory and honor" (Ps. 8:5). God takes the dust of the cocky know-it-all, driven achiever, perfectionistic, fearful soul and transforms it into maturity and Christlikeness.

4. Failure can be God's warning that I'm stuck in a rut and need to change something

I enjoy being successful. It feels good when things go smoothly. I like being comfortable. So do you. That's why when things are going well—when the waves aren't too high and the crises are manageable—we like to stay there. And that's okay, at least for a while.

The danger comes when we get too comfortable. A comfortable routine can easily turn into a rut. And a rut is nothing more than a grave with both ends kicked out. When the good feelings of safety and security become a sanctuary from life, we're in trouble.

Someone once said that a ship in the harbor is safe, but that isn't what ships were made for. Christ didn't die on the cross for us to hide in the harbor. He didn't sacrifice His life for us to play it safe. The low-risk life may seem cozy and secure, but when we spend our time and energy figuring out ways to detour around the risks of authentic living, it will zap our vision and lead to a life of mediocrity and stagnation.

James Russell Lowell said it well:

Life is a leaf of paper white,
Whereon each one of us may write,
His word or two . . . and then comes night.
Greatly begin, though thou have time but for a line,
Be that sublime.
Not failure, but low aim is crime.[4]

Our unhealthy response to failure is the epoxy glue that keeps us stuck in the rut of immaturity, irresponsibility, and mediocrity. The greatest mistake we can make is to be afraid to make a mistake. The danger doesn't lie in the failure. If I'm moving toward a goal and experience a failure, I can gain insight to get myself back on track from analyzing what went wrong. If I'm open to seeing what truth can be found in a negative experience or a criticism, I can learn from it and be stronger because of it.

Failure gets our attention and gives us an opportunity to reexamine ourselves. This can be more valuable than continuing to be safe and secure in things that are of secondary value. Failure can force us into reflection and conversation. It can help us get off the fences of life. It can push us beyond playing it safe.

In *A Preface to Christian Theology*, John Mackay described two kinds of people. He pictured the first group as people who are sitting on the high front balcony of an old Spanish house. They're watching travelers walk by on the road below. These "balconeers" listen to what the travelers have to say and comment on their conversations, how they're dressed, what they look like, and how they're walking. The watchers can discuss what the road is like, how old it is, why it was built in the first place, what shape it's in, where it goes, and what can be seen from different vantage points along it. However, they're the ones who play it safe. They're only onlookers and observers, not participants. Their observations are theoretical, not practical.

The second group are the "travelers." They're the ones who are actually on the road. They ask questions such as: how far should we go, which way should we go, and what do we need to make it? While there are some theoretical aspects to their journey, their concerns are primarily immediate and practical. They aren't hiding in the harbor. They're out hiking on the highway and not merely talking about it. The problems they face involve decision and action.

The balconeers enjoy deep discussions on the philosophical, theological, and existential implications of failure. The travelers are in the middle of it, trying to make some sense of it and muddle through it. They want help in not just getting through it, but in growing through it. The only ones who never lose are the ones who never compete. The only ones who never fail are the ones who never attempt anything. The late humorist and playwright George Ade once said, "Anyone can win, unless there happens to be a second entry."[5]

This book is for those who don't want to be balconeers. It's for men and women who want to risk moving beyond being hearers of the Word to aggressively pursuing becoming doers. God wants to help us move from failure to faith, from learned helplessness to learned hopefulness. This book is written to help show you how.

5. Failure is an essential part of success

One day, the president of a bank announced to one of his younger vice-presidents that he was going to retire and had selected the young man to replace him as president. The vice-president was overwhelmed by both the honor and the responsibility. After recovering from his surprise, he said, "Thank you, sir!" And then, in a very serious tone, he told the old man, "I've always admired your successful leadership. What's the key to being successful?"

The old man paused, put his hand to his chin, and replied, "Making good decisions."

The young man asked, "Where did you learn how to make good decisions?"

With a twinkle in his eye, the president replied, "By making bad ones."

You can't separate success from failure; they're two sides of the same coin. No one learns how to make right decisions without making wrong ones. No one is ever a real success who doesn't learn from failures. And in order to have failures, you have to show up and try.

Think about this. You always hear about Babe Ruth's 714 home runs, but you never hear that he also set the record for striking out in the process. You hear about Thomas Edison inventing the light bulb, but you rarely hear about the hundreds of failures that preceded that one success.

In August 1978, the first successful transatlantic balloon flight became a reality when Double Eagle II touched ground in a barley field in the small village of Miserey, France. But this successful flight wasn't made the first time it was attempted. From 1873 through 1978, thirteen attempts had been made. Each one ended in failure. After an unsuccessful attempt in 1977, in which Double Eagle ended up in Iceland, Double Eagle II was finally successful in making the historic six-day trip from Presque Isle, Maine, to Miserey, France.

What made the difference between the unsuccessful trip of Double Eagle and the successful one? One change was the addition of another man. The second major difference was experience. Maxie Anderson, one of the crew, put it this way: "I don't think that you can fly the Atlantic without experience, and that's one reason it hadn't been flown before. Success in any venture is just the intelligent application of failure."[6]

Now, please don't get me wrong. It's not that we should go out and *try* to fail. However, when those inevitable mistakes and setbacks do occur, we need to see them in light of the opportunity they provide us for growth.

As I fail I can learn, and so can others. A failure can be valuable to a number of people besides the one experiencing it. For instance, parents who can admit their own mistakes give their children a gift; as children realize that parents are human and fail, they learn that it's okay to fail and that failure is part of life — part of learning.

Many years ago, a young writer interviewed the legendary IBM president Thomas J. Watson. He was given some unusual advice by the industrialist: "It's not exactly my line," Watson said, "but would you like me to give you a formula for writing success? It's quite simple, really. Double your rate of failure."

Watson continued, "You're making a common mistake. You're thinking of failure as the enemy of success. But it isn't at all. Failure is a teacher — a harsh one perhaps, but the best."

Then he looked at the young writer and asked him a critical question: "You say you have a desk full of rejected manuscripts? That's great! Every one of those manuscripts was rejected for a reason. Have you pulled them to pieces looking for that reason?"

Arthur Gordon, the man who had interviewed Watson, went on to become a nationally known author and editor. He had originally gone to Watson for an interview, but Watson gave him something much more precious. He gave him a new perspective on failure.

"Somewhere inside me a basic attitude had shifted. A project turned down, a lot of rejected manuscripts—why, these were nothing to be ashamed of. They were rungs in a ladder—that was all. A wise and tolerant man had given me an idea. A simple idea, but a powerful one; if you can learn to learn from failure, you'll go pretty much where you want to go."[7]

Failures can leave many different scars—hurt feelings, wounded relationships, wasted potential, broken marriages, shattered ministries—but they can also be used by God to sharpen the mind, deepen the spirit, and strengthen the soul. Those people who have learned to view failure through God's eyes emerge with a softer heart, stronger character, and a fresh awareness of God's grace.

Are You Ready for the Challenge?

This book has been a long time in coming. Writing it has been both painful and pleasant. The *painful* part is that I've had to revisit some of the uglies in my own life—the times when, through stupidity, selfishness, and just plain sin, I let my God, my family, my friends, myself, and others down. I've been surprised to discover how the muck and mire of past mistakes can cling to my feet. I've been amazed at how easy it is to reexperience the powerful pain of past sins. Even though they've been forgiven, it's still painful. I'm even more amazed at how easy it is to stay stuck there.

The *pleasant* part is that in every situation, in every memory, through every illustration, I've seen the hand of God. I've seen His faithfulness to His promises. I've seen Romans 8:28 in action. Yes, He can cause all things to work together for good for those who love Him and are called according to His purpose.

Failure doesn't need to be futile. Nor does it need to be final. Someone once said that the difficulties of life are intended to make us better, not bitter. We can either groan through life or we can grow through it.

Have you ever felt stuck? Have you ever felt weak? Do you make mistakes? Do you ever feel like a failure? Do you want to grow and mature? Do you want a deeper experience of the Christian life? Would you like every day with Jesus to be sweeter than the day before? Read on. This book gives you a map through the minefield of failure. It was written for you!

Small Beginnings

1. What messages did you receive about failure as you were growing up?
2. What messages did you receive about yourself when you failed?
3. What's your immediate response to failure?
4. What's your immediate response to others when they fail?
5. Have you spent most of your life as a "balconeer" or as a "traveler"?

2. Why Spiritual People Fail

I can't do it!"

"I'll never get it right."

"I've tried before, and I blew it. Why should I try again?"

"It's just too hard. I quit!"

Have any of those phrases ever passed your lips? Have any such thoughts ever crossed your mind? They have mine. I can't count the number of times I've felt like quitting.

I remember as a young Christian walking along a Southern California beach feeling frustrated and hopeless. I had recently returned from a church camp. Once again I had recommitted my life to Christ. I promised God that I would have a "quiet time" every morning and that I would "flee youthful lusts." I was as sincere as I could be. I knew in my heart of hearts that this time, I really meant it and things would be different.

But in less than two weeks, I had missed several of my quiet times. I had failed to flee youthful lusts as quickly as I should have. Once again, I had allowed myself to yield to temptation and let God down. Once again, I was a failure.

All the familiar labels of self-condemnation came to my mind. I told myself I was weak, worthless, slow, stupid, a loser, and a fraud. I felt flawed, frustrated, and as spiritually anemic and immature as ever. I was ready to give up on myself, and I couldn't figure out why God wasn't giving up on me too. He had given me so many opportunities to learn, so many chances to succeed. He had already forgiven so many mistakes. And yet, in spite of all my knowledge and experience, once again I had let Him down.

As I've gotten older, I've discovered that many Christians spend much of their lives in the doldrums of discouragement. Of course, that's just the place Satan loves to have us. Our eyes are off of Christ and on our failure. We become so preoccupied with what we have or haven't done that we lose sight of what He's done. Our discouragement can quickly turn into despair, and we figure, *What's the use? Why try? I'll never be the person God wants me to be.*

We begin to climb out of that pit when we understand why we fail so easily and often. For the past several years, I've surveyed hundreds of people of different genders, socioeconomic status, ethnic background, vocation, and denominational affiliation. My initial goal was to find the top ten reasons why people fail. It didn't take long before I had to expand it to the top twenty and then the top thirty. My initial conclusion was that there are as many reasons people fail as there are people.

However, I also believed there were some core conditions or errors that set us up for and made us more vulnerable to those surface causes. As I spent hours wading through the myriad of seemingly random reasons people had given for failure, a light suddenly came on. It wasn't just a 20-watt bulb, either; it was more like a 1,000-watt spotlight. I started to see some patterns emerge.

I discovered that most of the different reasons can be traced back to five root causes. And I realized that if we can understand these core causal factors and deal with them, with God's help we can eliminate a lot of unnecessary failure and pain. So in this chapter, I want to list the "big five" and help you understand how to deal with them.

1. Conditional Commitment to God

Paul closed the third chapter of his letter to the church at Ephesus with a prayer. In verse 19, he asked God to help them to "know this love that surpasses knowledge — that you may be filled to the measure of all the fullness of God."

When I first read that verse, I found it somewhat confusing. In fact, it seemed contradictory. Paul appears to be asking God to help us know a kind of love that surpasses knowledge. But think about it. If it surpasses our ability to know it, how can we possibly know it? Since the Bible doesn't contradict itself, however, I realized I needed to dig a bit deeper.

What I discovered is that Paul was talking about two different kinds of knowledge. The first kind involves a mere acquisition of facts and information. We can call this "head knowledge." The scribes and Pharisees pursued excellence in the acquisition of head knowledge. They knew the Law. They knew the prophets. They were even able to tell the wise men where to find the long-awaited Messiah. Yet this abundant wealth of information hadn't gone any deeper than their heads. When the Messiah came, they missed Him, and they eventually crucified Him.

The second kind of knowledge is one that moves through the head and penetrates the heart. It's an experiential and life-transforming knowledge. I like to call this "heart knowledge." Look at the life of Peter. He didn't just know *about* Jesus; he *knew* Him. That intimate love relationship had been forged through years of experience with Jesus, and Peter's experiences included numerous mistakes and failures.

I've always found it interesting that when Jesus approached Peter on the shores of the Sea of Galilee after His resurrection, He didn't bawl him out for playing Zorro and cutting off the servant's ear. Jesus didn't dump on Peter for denying Him. He didn't give him a lecture on the correct way to catch fish. Three different times Christ looked Peter in the eyes and asked him the simple question, "Do you love Me?"

Every day, Jesus is asking you and me that same question.

After thirty years of ministry, I've come to realize that our answer is the key factor that determines the direction of our day.

How important is that question? When one of the Pharisees asked Jesus, "Teacher, which is the greatest commandment in the Law?" He didn't skip a beat. His immediate reply was, "Love the Lord your God with all your heart and with all your soul and with all your mind" (Matt. 22:36-37).

In the second chapter of Revelation, John recorded a message to the church at Ephesus. Remember that Ephesus was an "all-star" church. The people took pride in being the most biblical church around. They were characterized by good deeds, hard work, and perseverance. They didn't tolerate wicked men. They tested those who claimed to be apostles. They had endured hardships and not grown weary.

In verse 4, however, we read, "Yet I hold this against you: You have forsaken your first love. Remember the height from which you have fallen! Repent and do the things you did at first" (Rev. 2:4-5a). What Jesus was saying is, "Hey, folks, I appreciate all your hard work. You're doing a lot of great stuff. But it's time to get back to the basics." They were proud to be known as the church of right thinking and right doing. But God said, "I'm more concerned about your heart."

In my own life, some of my times of greatest failure have been the times when I've been working the hardest at serving the Lord. Gradually I got my eyes on what I was doing and how well I was doing it and off of Him. And I've discovered that this tendency isn't unique to me. I've spoken with hundreds of believers, including many Christian leaders, who have told me they experience the same thing.

If you think back to some of your recent failures, you may be surprised to discover that one of the root causes was a lack of consistency and faithfulness in maintaining an intimate, growing love relationship with your Lord Jesus Christ. In the Sermon on the Mount, Jesus said, "Do not store up for yourselves treasures on earth, where moth and rust destroy, and where thieves break in and steal. But store up for yourselves treasures in heaven. . . . For where your treasure is, there your heart will be also" (Matt. 6:19-21). I'm convinced that when you allow anything, including serving Him, to become your treasure, you've taken the first step down the road to failure.

2. Restricted Reliance on God's Word

In the first chapter of Joshua, the new commander-in-chief was preparing his people to enter and conquer the Promised Land. They had just spent forty long years wandering around in the wilderness. They had been dreaming about this land that flowed with milk and honey. They were eager and ready.

Before they started their conquest, God reminded Joshua of His secret weapon. In verse 7 He exhorted him to "Be strong and very courageous. Be careful to obey all the Law My servant Moses gave you; do not turn from it to the right or to the left, that you may be successful wherever you go."

Did you catch that last part? God clearly linked their success with the degree to which they obeyed God's Word. As they chose to focus on what they knew to be true, if they didn't take any detours, they would have success. They had just come off a forty-year detour where a good time was had by *none.* Maybe they had learned something.

Just to make sure they got the point, He repeated His exhortation to focus and meditate on God's Word day and night: "Do not let this Book of the Law depart from your mouth; meditate on it day and night, so that you may be careful to do everything written in it. Then you will be prosperous and successful" (1:8). Whenever I read that passage, I can see God turning to Joshua and asking, "Any questions?"

In Romans 12:1-2, Paul talked about the importance of choosing to daily present all of what we have and are to God as a "living and holy sacrifice" (NASB). In the second part of verse 2, Paul told us that an essential part of the process by which we become conformed to Christ involves "the renewing of your mind."

The word *renew* means "to make like new; restore to freshness, vigor, or perfection; to make extensive changes in." Why is this so important? In Proverbs 23:7, we read that "as he thinks within himself, so is he" (NASB). What we fill our minds with, what we allow our minds to dwell on, will, to a great degree, influence what we do. As someone once said:

> We have never said or done an ungracious or un-Christlike word or action which was not first an ungracious and un-Christlike thought. We have never felt dislike or hate for a person without first of all thinking thoughts of dislike which have grown into hate. We have never committed a visible act of sin which has shamed us before others which was not first a shameful thought. We have never wronged another person without first wronging them in our thoughts. What we habitually think, will, sooner or later, manifest itself clearly in some visible expression of that thought.

There's a similar principle in Jeremiah 31:21: "Set up road signs; put up guideposts. Take note of the highway, the road that you take." Warren Wiersbe has observed that "wrong thinking leads to wrong feeling, and before long the heart and mind are pulled apart. . . . We must realize that thoughts are real and powerful, even though they cannot be seen, weighed, or measured."[1]

For years I knew the importance of God's Word. I had memorized hundreds of verses. I had a large theological library. I spent hours getting into the Word. But I spent comparatively little time allowing the Word to get into me. I spent hours preparing spiritual meals for others. But foolishly, I didn't spend much time partaking myself.

God was patient with me. He allowed me to do some stupid things. He used many different setbacks to help me get the message. I thought that if I was reading the Bible, that was enough. On the way home from work one day, however, I heard Chuck Swindoll say, "Bible teaching is not like nuclear fallout. Exposure to it does not equal absorption of it." It was like being hit in the face with a truth I had known for years but hadn't "seen."

I spent years planning my day around all the important things I needed to do *for* the Lord rather than putting first things first and starting the day *with* Him. For the past several years, I've started getting up early (for me) in the morning. You need to understand that I'm not a morning person. But God used a statement by the late Dietrich Bonhoeffer to change my perspective. Bonhoeffer observed,

> The entire day receives order and discipline when it acquires unity. This unity must be sought and found in morning prayer. Squandered time of which we are ashamed, temptations to which we succumb, weaknesses and lack of courage in work, disorganization and lack of discipline in our thoughts and in our conversation with other men, all have their origin most often in the neglect of morning prayer.[2]

If you've been stuck in the rut of making the same mistakes over and over, it's clear that what you've been doing isn't working. And in that case, the smart thing to do is to try something different. Have you been spending consistent and quality time listening for God's voice speaking through His Word?

3. Inadequate Understanding of Our Identity in Christ

In Romans 12:3, Paul warned us, "Do not think of yourself more highly than you ought, but rather think of yourself with sober judgment, in accordance with the measure of faith God has given you." Satan doesn't really care whether we think too highly of ourselves or too lowly. His only concern is to keep us from seeing ourselves the way God sees us. He will do anything to keep us from understanding what it means to be "in Christ."

When we take our eyes off the cross and begin to think too highly of ourselves, we become self-centered and narcissistic. We run the risk of becoming legends in our own minds. It's like the man who wrote:

I love myself, I think I'm grand;
I go to the movies and I hold my hand.
I put my arm around my waist,
And when I get fresh I slap my face.

The people in the Bible rarely fell on their weak points; they fell on their strong ones. Over time, unguarded strength becomes a double weakness. Those places where we perceive ourselves to be the strongest are often the places where we're least likely to be prepared for a battle. Gordon MacDonald has made the powerful observation that "almost every personal defeat begins with our failure to know ourselves, to have a clear view of our capabilities (negative and positive), our propensities, our weak sides."[3]

There's a temptation to look at our strengths and allow them to blind us to the significance of our weaknesses. Samson did it. Saul did it. David did it. We do it. How does it work? It's like picking up a pair of binoculars and looking at our strengths and our sacrifices of time, resources, and self through the end that magnifies. Then we turn the binoculars around and look at our weaknesses. Suddenly and most conveniently, our laziness, selfishness, compromises, and bad habits of mind or action appear distant and small.

The opposite mistake is to think too lowly of ourselves. Some Christians confuse this with humility, but there's a big difference. We fall into this trap when we focus on what *we've* done rather than what *He* has done. When we dwell on our mistakes and failures, our minds aren't on Him. What we begin to see isn't exactly a pretty picture. It doesn't take long before we get discouraged and want to quit.

When we look at our identity, it's critical that we start at the cross. If we've confessed our sins and asked Jesus Christ into our hearts as our Savior and Lord, we've been born again. Now, because of the completed work of Jesus, all of us who have believed in Him have many strengths. We've been justified and are completely forgiven (see Rom. 5:1); we're free from condemnation (see Rom. 8:1-4); we're the righteousness of God in Christ (see 2 Cor. 5:21) and are partakers of the divine nature (see 2 Peter 1:4); we've received the Spirit of God into our lives (see 1 Cor. 2:12); we've been baptized into the body of Christ (see 1 Cor. 12:13); we've been given the mind of Christ (see 1 Cor. 2:16); and we have direct access to God through the Spirit (see Eph. 3:12).

But while we have many strengths, we still have some weaknesses. When we become new men and women in Christ, it doesn't mean the flesh magically disappears. It does mean we're new people with new resources to combat the flesh. But we need to be combat-ready. We must know who the enemy is, how he works, what our new resources are, and how to use them.

When Satan tempted Adam and Eve, he attacked them on three fronts: the lust of the flesh, the lust of the eyes, and the pride of life. When Satan tempted Jesus in the wilderness, he appealed to Him on three fronts: the lust of the flesh, the lust of the eyes, and the pride of life. Guess what? Satan is consistent. When he attacks us, he hits us in the same three areas. John wrote, "Do not love the world or anything in the world. If anyone loves the world, the love of the Father is not in him. For everything in the world—the cravings of sinful man, the lust of his eyes and the boasting of what he has and does—comes not from the Father but from the world. The world and its desires pass away, but the man who does the will of God lives forever" (1 John 2:15-17).

4. A Cavalier Attitude toward Temptation

Temptation means "to put to the test." Remember that temptation is one of the main weapons in Satan's arsenal against us.

But what he has designed for evil, our God can use for good. God allows us to be tempted for many reasons. Temptation can provide the fire that can bring the alloys and impurities of our lives to the surface (see 1 Peter 1:6-7). As we allow God to remove them, we can become "pure gold." Temptation can help us identify our weaknesses, point us toward new areas for growth, drive us to the cross, fortify our faith, increase our trust in Him, and help us, by His grace, to strengthen virtue.

Be assured that the experience of temptation does *not* mean you're a failure. An occupational hazard of being a Christian is that you will be tempted. It isn't a sin. In fact, in some ways you should be encouraged by the fact that you experience temptation. As John Vianney has stated, "The greatest of all evils is *not* to be tempted, because there are then grounds for believing that the devil looks upon us as his property."[4]

Every one of us is vulnerable to temptation, because we still have some of the old patterns of thinking and acting that we had before we were saved. In many cases, those ways of responding have become automatic. Due to repetition, they became so deeply ingrained that we aren't aware of them. They become likely "target areas" for the adversary. After knowing Jesus, Peter still struggled with self-control, James and John still had anger problems, and Paul still wrestled with doing what he didn't want to do and not doing what he wanted to do.

Jesus warned His disciples to "watch and pray so that you will not fall into temptation. The spirit is willing, but the body is weak" (Matt. 26:41). Peter warned us to "gird your minds for action" (1 Peter 1:13, NASB). When you gird, or prepare, your mind, you not only anticipate conflict, but you're also prepared for it. Then you're much less likely to be caught off guard by a "sneak attack."

When the great king and mighty warrior David allowed himself to be caught off guard, it changed the rest of his life. In 2 Samuel 11, we find that his affair started out so innocently. He went for a stroll on the roof of his palace and noticed Bathsheba bathing. He observed that she was a fine-looking woman. So far, no problem. The fact that David noticed Bathsheba's beauty was not in itself sin. Unfortunately, he didn't stop there.

He next made a huge mistake. He continued to dwell on Bathsheba. He began to entertain fantasies about her. He probably visualized himself being with her. Certainly he was smart enough to know that with every second, he was increasing his vulnerability. Surely the still, small voice within him was telling him this was wrong. But he didn't listen. He didn't take the initiative to do the right thing. He made a choice to compromise. He refused to submit his thought life to what he knew to be true.

David could have chosen *not* to dwell on these immoral fantasies. He could have chosen to capture those thoughts, give them to God, and immediately replace them with healthy thinking. In James 4:7, we're told to resist the devil and he will flee from us. David not only didn't resist, he even sent his messengers to find out who she was. Even after he found out Bathsheba was a married woman, he still chose to have her brought to him.

That's the way temptation works. The initial temptation is rarely to sin. It's more often a temptation to linger too long. And that becomes the first link in a chain of seemingly innocent choices that lead to destruction. From the clear teaching of Scripture as well as from my own experience, I can tell you that the longer you linger, the sooner you'll stumble.

If we don't *immediately* identify the sinful thoughts and take them captive to what we know to be true — if we don't *immediately* replace the wrong thinking with right thinking — we'll become so weak that we don't care what we do. That is, we don't care until after we've sinned and begun to taste the bitter consequences. If you want to know how bitter they can be, read 2 Samuel 12.

As David Swartz has written, "Temptation is the striptease of sin. In seducing our hearts, it promises satisfaction and fulfillment that never genuinely materializes in the way originally anticipated. One thing is promised, another is delivered. Temptation may be alluring, but sin always exacts a price for that shallow come-on."[5]

I recently came across a humorous "CATHY" cartoon strip that illustrates what can happen when we don't immediately take every thought captive. Once again Cathy is struggling with her diet. Once again she has good intentions.

Frame 1: I will take a drive but won't go near the grocery store.
Frame 2: I will drive by the grocery store but will not go in.
Frame 3: I will go in the grocery store but will not walk down the aisle where the Halloween candy is on sale.
Frame 4: I will look at the candy but not pick it up.
Frame 5: I will pick it up but not buy it.
Frame 6: I will buy it but not open it.
Frame 7: Open it but not smell it.
Frame 8: Smell it but not taste it.
Frame 9: Taste it but not eat it.
Frame 10: Eat, Eat, Eat, Eat, Eat![6]

Here's my question. Go back and read over each statement. At what point did Cathy lose the battle? Many people would say frame 10. Some might say frame 9. If you guessed frame 2, you're correct. When she made the seemingly innocent decision to drive by the grocery store, the battle was lost.

In the cartoon, Cathy's struggle is humorous. However, I've worked with many real people whose response to temptation was similar. With each rationalization, with each justification, they became weaker and weaker. Once we allow ourselves to entertain unhealthy thoughts, once we choose not to take those thoughts captive, once we start to rationalize and justify our desires or actions, once we choose to compromise what we know to be true . . . the party is over. The battle has been lost.

The price of not *immediately* "taking every thought captive to the obedience of Christ" (2 Cor. 10:5, NASB) is too high for any of us to pay. I'll have more to say about this in the chapter on moral and ethical failure. But for now remember this: When you fail to flee, you will fail to flourish, and you will succeed at failing.

5. The Failure to Put First Things First

This particular launch of the space shuttle *Challenger* was unique. It was the first time ordinary citizens could participate in a NASA mission. But only seventy-three seconds into its flight, it blew apart. It exploded right before our eyes. And then we watched in horror as the trails of smoke and debris fell toward the ocean.

The investigation into the cause of the debacle revealed an even greater tragedy. The explosion was avoidable. It was caused by poor judgment and flawed materials. A group of top managers failed to listen to the warnings of engineers down the line. They had been warned of the questionable reliability of certain parts of the booster rocket under conditions of abnormal stress. Those who were responsible for making the final decision were sure that they knew what was best. They decided to go ahead with the launch schedule. They were wrong. The ultimate conclusion is that the disaster was caused by pride.

A little O-ring, a circular rubber seal designed to keep gases from leaking at the joints during the launch, had performed adequately on all previous flights. But on this particular day, the temperature had dropped below the freezing point. The engineers were concerned that under such conditions the O-rings could become brittle and allow pressurized fuel to leak out. And that's exactly what happened.

Historians tell us that the captain of the *Titanic* was warned six times to head south because there were icebergs ahead. But he was on the *Titanic*, and it was supposedly invincible. He figured he didn't need to worry about a few little icebergs.

There have been times in my life when, like the captain of the

Titanic, I ignored the warnings of icebergs. My previous mistakes and setbacks were God's warnings that I didn't heed. Looking back, it's resplendently clear that circumstances had been deteriorating for some time. Although over the previous years there had been many clues that something was wrong, I hadn't "gotten the message" of my "minor mistakes."

It's easy to look at the piles on our desks and overfull schedules as markers of our significance or popularity. But they're more likely signs of our fear of being insignificant and our inability to set boundaries and put first things first. A need to feel important, to shift our awareness from the deeper issues of becoming to performing, can turn a busy life into a frantic life. That leads to obscure values, lopsided priorities, and a significantly increased vulnerability to the failure that we're so desperately trying to avoid.

I used to work longer and harder to do whatever I thought needed to be done to meet the expectations of others. Now I find that getting up in the morning, having time in the Word, and making time for a Sabbath rest allows me to gain a fresh perspective. When I wait upon the Lord, He does renew my strength. He gives me the strength each day to accomplish what He wants accomplished.

In Isaiah 40:31 we're told, "Those who hope in the Lord will renew their strength. They will soar on wings like eagles; they will run and not grow weary, they will walk and not be faint." There have been times in my life when I've felt as if I were mounting up with the wings of a finch or a parakeet rather than the wings of an eagle, but that's because I was trying to do things in my own strength.

John Lord wisely observed, "Failure, once it hits, finds an easy mark in people whose commitments to work have caused them to sacrifice the very resources — individual and social — that would have enabled them to keep their equilibrium."[7]

In his book *Integrity: How I Lost It and My Journey Back*, Richard Dortch talked about how easy it is to stray from the presence of the Lord, even when you're in His work. He told how he allowed the busyness of Christian ministry to slowly and subtly seduce him away from putting first things first. It contributed to the collapse of Jim Bakker's PTL ministry. It cost Dortch his integrity and reputation. It tarnished the name of Christ. In fact, it gave all Christian ministries a black eye.

> I didn't experience failure because of a lack of ability. I had superior numbers most of my life. The problem is that I didn't make a fight of standing for what I knew was the best. I didn't [experience] failure because of idleness. It wasn't because I or anyone else at PTL was lazy. We worked hard, and we failed not from ignorance or inability or from idleness, but because we were too busy. We cannot deny it. The secondary so absorbed us that we neglected the primary.
>
> The sin that we must fear the most is not the sin of vicious wrong-doing, it is the sin of choosing the second best. And that is where our integrity fails. If we spend most of our time doing trivial things, we rob ourselves of doing something better. So much of our time is spent in good things, but perhaps not the best. Often we were engaged in great, stressful, straining trivialities. Perhaps they were not especially harmful, but the calamity of it all is that they so absorbed us, we didn't have time for the highest. It is so easy to become passionately involved in amusing ourselves. We were doing a thousand and one decent and good things; but while we were busy here and there, something of God slipped out of our lives and we didn't have the keen interest we should have in simply "knowing God," which should be our highest goal.[8]

Failure of many kinds is all too easy in this life. And when we get even a little careless about our relationship with God, that failure can extend to our spiritual experience. Even good people—a ministry leader like a Richard Dortch, for example—can make the mistakes outlined in this chapter. I've been trying to learn these lessons and apply them in my own daily walk so I don't fail unnecessarily. And I've also found it helpful to realize that failure typically involves a series of predictable phases through which we pass. We'll look at those phases and how to deal with each of them in the next chapter.

Small Beginnings

1. Recall a recent "season of success" or "season of setbacks." What was it like? What did you learn from it? What kinds of habits and disciplines contributed to your success? What kinds of behaviors and attitudes set you up for failure?
2. Take a moment to skim back through the chapter and reread the five core reasons for failure. Which one sticks in your mind as something God wants you to deal with now? Why?
3. Read Psalm 103. What's one principle in that passage that you can apply in your life today?

3. The Anatomy of Failure

'll never forget the time I learned the value of an accurate map. It was about twenty years ago. My sister Marsha and I had one week to explore the French countryside before we were to meet our parents for a family vacation. We were trying to find our way from Paris to Rheims. I say "trying" because we had already discovered that our map wasn't totally accurate. Besides that, we weren't sure where we were. But we were still having fun.

Then we got lost. I mean *really* lost. We had come to a fork in the road. The sign had two arrows pointing in two different directions, both indicating that the road led to Rheims. We decided to go to the right.

It was a beautiful day. The scenery was gorgeous. We were chatting happily until I noticed we were coming to another fork in the road. As we got closer, I saw a sign with two arrows pointing in two different directions. Both arrows indicated that the road led to Rheims.

Suddenly Marsha and I turned to each other and started laughing. We had just spent more than two hours going in a circle, ending up right back where we had started! It turned out that the right road was the wrong road. So we decided to do something different. We went to the left. And eventually we ended up at our intended destination.

I learned a lesson that day that I've never forgotten: If you want to get from one place to another and you don't know the way, it's helpful to have a map—an accurate map. But equally important is to know where you are on the map. If you don't know that, it will be difficult to figure out how to get to your destination.

When most of us are on the journey through failure, the last thing we think about is a map. Our tendency is to push the accelerator down as hard as we can and power through the pain as quickly as possible. But when you don't know where you're going, it rarely helps to go faster. Often, the faster you go, the more lost you'll become.

Failure was never intended to be a final destination. God wants to use it as a midpoint on the road to maturity. So in this chapter, I want to give you a road map to help you understand the inevitable journey through failure. My hope is that thus equipped, you'll be able to avoid being derailed by detours and going around in circles like so many others.

Failure comes in packages of all different sizes, shapes, weights, and colors, but all of them have one thing in common: They involve a sense of loss that affects several areas of life. It doesn't matter whether the loss is one of money, hope, prestige, confidence, integrity, job, or relationships. When it hits, it can affect every dimension of who we are.

Even if our failure hasn't become obvious, there are often subtle indications that something is wrong. What are they? The first warning sign is often changes in the body. Our appetite may increase. During difficult times, it's easy for food to become a kind of anesthetic to ease our pain. Exercise may decrease or stop totally. There may be an increased vulnerability to alcohol. There may also be changes in our sexual behavior. Failure can produce either a decrease or an increase in sexuality.

We may also become aware of changes in our ability to think. We may find that our processing is slowed, it's harder to focus, we have difficulty concentrating, our short-term memory is impaired, we're more confused, and it's hard to think about anything but the problem. We may also discover that our decisions aren't quite as good as usual. It can feel as if the whole world is aware of our failure.

It's most often in the area of our emotions that we experience the greatest fluctuation. They run the gamut from strong, intense, and overwhelming to weeks or months of not feeling anything at all. The emotions people go through in times of deep emotional upheaval such as death, divorce, or spiritual or career failure are very similar.

The only difference between people is what we *do* with those emotions and how quickly we allow God to help us get through the cycle of feelings. And since failure always involves some kind of loss, the process of moving through failure involves stages that are similar to the process of dealing with grief. Let's look at each of those typical stages.

Phase 1: The Crisis Phase

I love Colorado. It's a majestic state, and there are many beautiful places to visit. One of my family's favorite drives is between Estes Park and Loveland. Over the centuries, the Big Thompson River has carved a pathway through the steep granite walls of the Big Thompson Canyon. There are numerous spots along the way to stop and enjoy the lovely sights and the relaxing sound of the water as it winds its way down the mountain. For generations, people from around the world have enjoyed camping, fishing, and just driving in this scenic canyon.

However, on August 1, 1976, the soothing serenity of this mountain scene turned into a nightmare. That evening, a torrent of water began issuing from the deceptively named Dry Gulch. In only a few hours, a deluge of rain dumped eleven and a half inches of water into the river and its tributaries. At its crest, the flood achieved a volume four times that of any previously recorded flood.

Hundreds of campers, hikers, and sightseers were caught totally by surprise. Terrified refugees who had managed to climb high enough on the canyon walls to escape harm watched helplessly as camp trailers, houses, cars, exploding propane tanks, and human bodies rushed by in the torrent. By morning, 144 people were presumed to be dead, and $80 million in damage had been sustained.

Whether it builds gradually or crashes in around us like a flash flood, when a crisis hits, it can hit with a vengeance. In recalling a crisis experience in his own life, Gordon MacDonald wrote:

> I will never forget those first days. It was almost impossible to ward off the feeling that life was over, that all the brightness and joy that we had known for more than forty-five years had come to a screeching halt.
>
> Our worlds were broken. A dream had turned into a nightmare of loss, humiliation, anger, and a sense of a very dark future. There was the terrible realization that many who had trusted me were now disillusioned. There was the knowledge that some people were talking, with or without a knowledge of the facts.
>
> At one point I felt as though the ground was opening beneath me! Like if I were to look down the world was going to swallow me up![1]

MacDonald isn't alone in his dramatic description of the crisis phase. Others have told me:

> "I felt like I was in a free fall. But I didn't have a parachute!"
> "It was a strange sensation. I sort of felt as though the world was somehow less real, like I was disconnected, except of course when it came crashing in on me. It was that kind of alternating experience: Sometimes I was 'out of it'; sometimes I was in the middle of it; but I could never get away from it."
> "There was this growing sense of powerlessness."

"I'm one of those people who always have options. But when I hit the steel-reinforced wall of failure, all my options and opportunities for constructive action disappeared."

"When the reality of my failure hit me, it was like a part of me left myself and was forced to watch myself wallow in my own helplessness."

"I pride myself on being a proactive person. But when I discovered myself in the middle of my failure, I became so drained and discouraged that it was even hard to react."

The crisis might be something everyone would view as major, or it may be a combination of things so small that nobody would understand why you're "blowing it all out of proportion" and allowing it to affect you so. It doesn't matter. Whether it comes from within or without, whether it's big or small, once the sharp blade of failure cuts through the thin crust of your successful, "everything is fine" topsoil, there's no turning back.

One middle-aged man said, "It seemed like suddenly everything started falling apart. Usually I was able to pull together some resources, summon some inner strength, and pull off some minor miracle to keep things together. This time my well-worn tactics didn't work. Things just started moving faster and faster, and everything caught up with me at once. And for the first time in my life, there was absolutely nothing I could do about it."

I used to think that the intensity of the crisis was due to the magnitude of the failure, but that's not necessarily true. A person's real failure may have been quite small. But if his or her *perceived* failure is great, the intensity of the crisis will be great as well.

Whether it builds gradually or sneaks up on you, the key to the crisis phase is to remember that it isn't terminal. It's only the opening act of the process. Just within the crisis phase, in fact, we move through six stages that mirror the stages in the grieving process.

1. Shock

The first reaction to sudden loss is disbelief, shock, and numbness. We seem to feel a spiraling confusion as we tumble into the experience of a major failure. It throws us off balance. It turns things upside down. Nothing seems normal. Those who have fallen flat on their face will usually say that they were surprised, unprepared, and sick with themselves after it happened.

In the shock phase, we may find ourselves questioning things we've always believed to be true. In his best-selling book *When Bad Things Happen to Good People*, Rabbi Harold Kushner gave a vivid description of how the illness and early death of his son threw him into a crisis of faith. The beliefs he had taught and been taught — of a gracious God who could be relied on to rescue him or those he loved — seemed to vanish in the painful reality of his loss.

> Like most people, my wife and I had grown up with an image of God as an all-wise, all-powerful parent figure who would treat us as our earthly parents did, or even better. If we were obedient and deserving, He would reward us. If we got out of line, He would discipline us, reluctantly but firmly. He would protect us from being hurt or from hurting ourselves, and He would see to it that we got what we deserved in life.
>
> Like most people, I was aware of the human tragedies that darkened the landscape — the young people who died in car crashes, the cheerful, loving people wasted by crippling diseases, the neighbors and relatives whose retarded or mentally ill children people spoke of in hushed tones. But that awareness never drove me to wonder about God's justice, or to question His fairness. I assumed that He knew more about the world than I did.
>
> Then came that day in the hospital when the doctor told us about Aaron and explained what progeria meant. It contradicted everything I had been taught. I could only repeat

over and over again in my mind, "This can't be happening. It is not how the world is supposed to work." Tragedies like this were supposed to happen to selfish, dishonest people whom I as a rabbi would then try to comfort by assuring them of God's forgiving love. How could it be happening to me, to my son, if what I believed about the world was true?[2]

2. Denial and Blame

As we begin the slow recovery from the immediate shock, our next response is most often one of denial. We find ourselves saying things like "This isn't really happening." "It's not as bad as it seems." "Somehow something will happen to clear all of this up."

At this point, we have a heightened vulnerability to look for distractions. Anything that can help us avoid looking at the problem will do. It might be working longer hours, taking on a new project, eating more, exercising more, or even spending more time acquiring "head knowledge" in Bible study.

We don't make a conscious choice to deny the reality of our circumstances. But there's a part of us that's overwhelmed by the pain, the humiliation, the stark reality of our plight. And our response is to keep our heads above water any way we can—even if for a brief time it involves denying we're *in* deep water.

For most of us, the denial process includes a search for someone to blame. If we can find someone to blame, if it wasn't all our fault, the failure isn't quite so bad. If "they" had done their job, if they had done something different, if they had caught things earlier, this never would have happened.

The problem with the blame response is that it robs us of the opportunity to identify and take responsibility for our part of the problem. If we miss that step, we're also going to miss what God wants to teach us. And if we allow that to happen, we've really failed. We've turned the situation into a double loss.

3. Withdrawal

As Carole Hyatt and Linda Gottlieb wrote in *When Smart People Fail:*

> Failure is the most democratic of all clubs, admitting old and young, rich and poor, black and white, chief executive officers and simple clerks. About the only thing its members have in common is their secrecy about belonging. Think of what a national convocation of all eligible members of the Failure Club would look like: millions of people crowded tightly together in thousands of rooms across America—all looking down at their feet.[3]

As the pain and pressure grow, so do the tendencies toward withdrawal. I remember seasons of failure in my own life when I felt profoundly isolated. Oh, I tried to keep up a good front. I told my friends that I was fine, that I knew God would use this setback. I minimized and understated the situation. But inside I was dying. I wanted to run and hide.

The problem with withdrawal is that we lose the opportunity to "pool" our failures and learn from each other. We lose the strength, encouragement, and perspective that friends can give us. Think about it. We rarely discuss our failures until after we're through them. In fact, I've met many people who have *never* talked about their failures to anyone else.

4. Fear and Anger

Fear and anger are necessary and can be a very healthy part of the growth process as long as we don't get stuck there. The more we withdraw and isolate, the more vulnerable we become to fear. Healthy fear focuses on a real and specific threat, alerting us to danger. It's a God-given emotion. But when we focus on the fear and allow it to overwhelm us, when we feed the fear and it becomes all we see, it's no longer serving the function for which God designed it. This unhealthy fear can become paralyzing. If we let our fear get the best of us, it can also turn easily into panic, which can be incapacitating.

Anger is a secondary emotion that's usually caused by a primary emotion such as fear, hurt, or frustration. It's not uncommon to experience all three of these and thus feel angry. When we're in the early stages of failure, we may feel powerless, but anger-energy can give us power. We may have been unfocused; anger can give us focus. We may have been afraid to act; anger can give us the confidence to act.

5. Shame

Whenever our performance falls short of our expectations, we experience some degree of shame. Shame tells us we're fallen, flawed, and finite. In itself, that's not bad. All of us are flawed in some way. We all have strengths and weaknesses. Romans 3:23 tells us that "all have sinned and fall short of the glory of God." As we're able to identify our blind spots and weaknesses, we can work on those areas, and God can help us develop creative alternatives.

Shame becomes toxic, however, when we allow it to define who we are. Once shame becomes the basis for our identity, it becomes dehumanizing. Allowing what we've done to obscure what He has done for us gets us in ever deeper trouble.

Toxic shame involves a sense of terminal worthlessness and hopelessness. It says that our basic nature is inadequate and unlovable and always will be. This is who we are, and we'll never be different.

Toxic shame causes people to become inordinately self-conscious. When we forget who we are in Christ and become focused on our failures, it's hard to see anything else. Thus, toxic shame can silence us and deepen our withdrawal. Because of our fear of saying or doing the wrong thing, because of our fear of looking stupid and being ridiculed, because of our fear of even being noticed, we don't say or do anything at all.

Further, toxic shame can keep us from trusting others and developing close, intimate relationships. Since we see ourselves as terminally worthless, it follows that if others ever see us as we really are, they'll reject us. Rather than face the possibility of that painful humiliation, we keep a wall around us so that no one will ever see the real self.

Toxic shame can render us powerless. Rather than seeking God's direction for our lives and moving out in a proactive sense of confidence, we become reactive. We spend our time reading our environment and trying to figure out what's expected of us and how we need to respond to stay out of trouble and gain someone's approval. Toxic shame keeps us from becoming the unique man or woman God designed us to be (see Ps. 139).

If we get stuck in the pothole of toxic shame, it can cause our lives to become characterized by remorse, self-hate, accident proneness, jealousy, bitterness, resentment, hopelessness, helplessness, frustration, punishment seeking, depression, irrational fears, and behaviors such as lying, stealing, and physical violence.

There have been times when the shame and self-doubt that overwhelmed me following a personal failure were so great that I didn't want to attempt anything for God. I didn't want to be a leader. I didn't want to be up front. I didn't want anybody to expect anything from me.

At this point of the healing process it's critical that we remember the power of God's promises and the name of Jesus. On more than one occasion, God has used the inspired music of Bill and Gloria Gaither to turn my eyes back to Him:

"He Touched Me"

Shackled by a heavy burden,
'Neath a load of guilt and shame,
Then the hand of Jesus touched me,
And now I am no longer the same.
He touched me, oh, He touched me.
And, oh, the joy that floods my soul.
Something happened and now I know,
He touched me and made me whole.[4]

During your deepest and darkest hour the God who promised to never leave or forsake you is right there with you, wanting to touch you, heal your wounds, and make you whole.

6. *Depression and Despair*

Following any kind of loss, most people's grief runs its course in a reasonable length of time. There are places in the grief process, however, where it's easy for us to get stuck. One of those is shame. Another is depression.

Abraham Lincoln became so depressed following the death of his first love, Ann Rutledge, that his friends feared he would commit suicide and took away his knives and razors. Winston Churchill was periodically beset with what he called his "black dog" of depression. Great writers such as Dostoevsky and Edgar Allan Poe were also victims of severe depression.

Depression is a God-given emotion that can be an indication that we've lost something important to our health and well-being and need to take positive steps to restore it. Depression affects millions of people every year. I've heard statistics suggesting that one out of every seven individuals will need professional help for depression at some time in life. It has been estimated that industry in America loses $4 to $6 billion of productivity annually due to the effects of depression that's either unacknowledged or untreated.

Medical experts tell us that depression is the world's number one public health problem. In fact, depression is so widespread that many consider it to be the common cold of psychiatric disturbances. But, as Dr. David Burns notes, there is a grim difference between depression and a cold. Depression can kill you. In spite of the billions of antidepressant drugs and tranquilizers that have been dispensed during the past several decades, the suicide rate has continued to grow.[5]

It's unfortunate that some Christians find it hard to admit they experience depression. Many have the wrong idea that the Bible teaches that Christians should not be depressed, and so depression must be a sin. Instead of identifying their depression and using the resources God has given us for dealing with it, they prefer to deny their depression or minimize it by saying they're sad, discouraged, or just feeling a bit low.

D. Martyn Lloyd-Jones had some helpful insights about depression. He wrote:

> It is interesting to notice the frequency with which this particular theme is dealt with in the Scriptures, and the only conclusion to be drawn from that is that it is a very common condition. It seems to be a condition which has afflicted God's people right from the beginning, for you find it described and dealt with in the Old Testament and in the New. That in itself would be sufficient reason for drawing your attention to it, but I do so also because it seems in many ways to be the peculiar trouble with many of God's people and the special problem troubling them at this present time. . . . It is very sad to contemplate the fact that there are Christian people who live the greater part of their lives in this world in such a condition.[6]

When Christ was here on earth, He experienced and expressed the full range of human emotions, including depression. Look, for example, at the account of His feelings in the Garden of Gethsemane in Matthew 26:36-38:

> Then Jesus went with them to a place called Gethsemane, and He told His disciples, "Sit down here while I go over yonder and pray." And taking with Him Peter and the two sons of Zebedee, He began to show grief and distress of mind and was deeply depressed. Then He said to them, "My soul is very sad and deeply grieved, so that I am almost dying of sorrow. Stay here and keep awake and watch with Me" (AMP).

Jesus knew full well what He was facing. He had known from the beginning of time that His experience on earth would end at the cross. From a human perspective, He was facing the prospect of the excruciating physical pain of the crucifixion. From a spiritual perspective, He was facing separation from His Father. These realities caused Him to experience depression. His depression didn't control Him, but it was there. He felt it and expressed it to His friends and to His Father.

One of the most effective ways to deal with depression is to admit it, embrace it, feel it, and allow ourselves to mourn. If the tears come, we should let them flow. That doesn't mean we're weak or emotional infants. It means we're human. During this phase, friends are an important source of support and comfort. If we experience a significant failure, we'll be surprised by two things—the friends who desert us and the friends who stick with us. We need to reach out for those who are faithful.

Phase 2: The Crossroads Phase

I believe it was Woody Allen who said, "More than any time in history, mankind faces a crossroads. One path leads to despair and utter hopelessness, the other to total extinction. Let us pray that we have the wisdom to choose correctly."

Several years ago, two world-class female athletes were competing in the Los Angeles Olympics. One was from America, the other from New Zealand. One wore the usual track shoes, and the other raced barefoot. Millions of viewers focused on their rivalry. The American was the sentimental favorite. The drama mounted as, for the first thousand meters, they matched each other stride for stride. Who would be the first to make her move? Who would win the gold?

Then suddenly, so quickly that the replay cameras couldn't determine what had happened, something went wrong. For some inexplicable reason, the American runner tripped and ended up sprawled out on the infield grass. But she didn't jump up. The television commentators wondered if she was hurt and couldn't get up. As the camera zoomed in on her, you could see the agony and anger of defeat deeply etched on her face. Years of discipline and denial as well as thousands of hours of training were down the drain.

That reminded me of another race I had seen several years earlier. In the classic movie *Chariots of Fire,* world-class runner Eric Liddell was in a group of runners getting ready to break for the lead. Suddenly he was thrown off balance and crashed onto the infield grass. The camera zoomed in for a slow-motion closeup as he lifted his head to see the other runners pulling away.

As I watched that scene, I wondered, *Will he get up? Will he try to finish the race?* I was sure there was no way. For Eric Liddell, that race was over.

I was wrong. Although he was covered with grass stains, dirt smudges, and bruises, he got back on the track. He began to run. He ran hard toward the now-distant pack of runners. And he not only finished the race—he won.

The Bible describes the Christian life as a race. In 1 Corinthians 9:24, Paul asked, "Do you not know that in a race all the runners run, but only one gets the prize? Run in such a way as to get the prize." In Hebrews 12:1, we're exhorted to "run with perseverance the race marked out for us."

The most difficult part of the race of life can be when failure forces us facedown on the infield grass. We're hurt. We've been set back. Others have gotten ahead of us. It's tempting to lie down and give up. *Why try to get back up?* we're tempted to think. *It won't do any good.*

When we come face-to-face with failure, we're at a crossroads. One of the main challenges in this stage of failure is to decide what we're going to do about what has happened. We can choose one of three responses: the fight response, the flight response, or the faith response. Let's take a closer look at each one.

The Fight Response

Those who choose the fight response choose to stay in the blame mode. "It's not my fault. Everyone else is a loser, a jerk. It's somebody else's fault—my spouse, my kids, my boss, my toilet training." It's incredible to hear some of the excuses people use to fight their responsibility in their failure.

This isn't anything new. Cover-ups started in the Garden of

Eden, and they continue in most people's response to failure. Richard Nixon, for example, rather than own his responsibility, chose the fight response, and the tragic story of Watergate overshadows many of the good things he did.

The Flight Response

If you choose the flight response, you'll kick yourself, beat yourself up, and become consumed by the problem. It will feel as if you're stuck in a tailspin, cycling between shame and depression. You'll hear yourself saying things like,

"I'm a loser."

"I'm a jerk."

"It's always my fault."

"I'm just a zit on the face of life."

"I'll never be able to change."

"I deserve everything I get. In fact, I'm so bad that I probably deserve more."

What we deserve because we're sinful human beings is very different from who God has declared us to be because of the completed work of Christ on the cross. Satan loves for us to focus on the first. Dorothy Sayers, with her characteristically keen insight, observed:

All of us, perhaps, are too ready, when our behaviour turns out to have appalling consequences, to rush out and hang ourselves. Sometimes we do worse, and show an inclination to go and hang other people. Judas, at least, seems to have blamed nobody but himself, and St. Peter, who had a minor betrayal of his own to weep for, made his act of contrition and waited to see what came next. What came next for St. Peter and the other disciples was the sudden assurance of who God was, and with it the answer to all the riddles.[7]

How does flight manifest itself? Through procrastination or by burying ourselves in our work, ministry, family, friends, or hobby. We hide by ignoring the crisis and pretending it didn't happen. But if we don't learn the lessons pain can teach us, we'll spend our lives trying to figure out ways to experience only a very narrow band of the rainbow that God designed life to be. We try to go around pain rather than growing through it. And in the process, we miss life.

Then maybe, toward the end of our lives, a little light comes on, and we realize (almost too late) that some of the things we avoided were the things God allowed to add depth and breadth to our lives. Our desire to play it safe has caused our lives to be a one-note symphony.

When you come to the crossroads of failure, you can do what Marsha and I did on our trip through the French countryside. You can take the wrong turn and end up going around in circles. If you choose the fight or flight response, that's exactly what will happen. However, there's a third option.

The Faith Response
It's a cliché that failure isn't a closed door but an opportunity. That's easy to say when everything is going great. But when you're in the middle of a whopper of a failure, when things have come crashing down around you, one of the statements you're *least* likely to make is, "Wow! Thank You, Lord, for this great opportunity. I can't believe how fortunate I am to be able to learn something like this at my age. Am I blessed or what?"

Failures are a turning point in our relationship with God, ourselves, and others. The word *crisis* means "decision." The decision we make at the crossroads phase of failure will reflect what we believe about God, and it will determine *if* we'll grow, *how* we'll grow, *where* we'll grow — or whether we'll continue to do things our way and miss what God has purposed for our lives.

At this point, we need to remind ourselves that failure is ultimately an *evaluation* of an event. It defines a stage. It's not fatal. It's not final. It's not a condemnation of character. Nor is it a contagious social disease. Everything we shut our eyes to, run away from, deny, denigrate, or despise serves to defeat us in the end. But God can take what feels humiliating or painful and use it as a source of beauty, joy, and strength. *If we look at it through the eyes of faith, every failure is a golden opportunity.*

Failure brings us to a crossroads where we can either focus on the failure or focus on God's grace and decide to learn from it. We can choose the faith response and move on to the growth phase, or we can set ourselves up for another inevitable crisis. If failure is a bondage maker, the faith response can be a bondage breaker! The choice we make tells the world in large part who we are and what kind of people we'll become.

When Gordon MacDonald came face-to-face with the reality of a major failure, he reached out to some godly leaders for their counsel. His spiritual advisers challenged him and his wife, Gail, with this question: "Will you choose to dwell on the pain of your broken-world experience, or will you permit God to use the pain as an environment in which He can clearly speak to you about the things He sees as ultimately important? The choice is yours." MacDonald wrote:

> We were going to have to make a choice. . . . Would we fight the pain of the aftermath of my sin, or would we permit the pain to be part of the rebuilding process? It wasn't a one-time choice. We made it again and again as time passed. A score of ways could be found to bring back the pain. And each time the choice had to be made again. Would we fight the pain or permit it to be the environment in which God speaks? . . .
>
> During those dark hours I spent large quantities of time scanning the Scriptures. I looked at familiar, biblical biographies in a whole new light. What startled me more than anything else, however, was one insight regarding the great personalities of the Bible. Almost every one of them had experienced a broken-world moment. . . . I could hardly find an exception. Failures, sufferings, oppositions and oppressions, outright sins of great magnitude, sicknesses, rejections, marital and family catastrophes, and grave moments of spiritual crisis.

As I studied the record of these broken worlds, I found comfort. Others had gone through my pain; others had experienced the same feelings I knew; others were at one time or another as undependable as I saw myself to be; others had received great grace and healing as I hoped to receive. And, finally, others had gone on to the greatest moments of their service to God.[8]

A turning point in the change process comes when we stick up our hands, turn to God, and say, "I give! I can't do it on my own. I want to begin the process of surrendering my need for control. I'm willing to do what You want me to do."

If you feel as though your whole world has been shattered into a thousand pieces, there's still hope. The jigsaw puzzle can be put back together again. It was, in part, the experience of failure that led Bill and Gloria Gaither to write "Something Beautiful," whose lyrics are in part recorded in chapter 1.

When you're at the crossroads, you're face-to-face with confusion, brokenness, and strife. As the Gaithers put it, you're standing amid the ruins of dreams that have faded, castles that have crumbled, and fortunes that have disappeared. It's your choice: Stay stuck or grow. Keep on doing what doesn't work, or surrender to God and trust Him to show you a different direction.

Unfortunately, the small failures are easy to rationalize away. They may not be strong-enough medicine to purge from your mind those old habits of the heart. But that's one reason I wrote this book. If you will allow God to teach you how to learn from the small failures, you can save yourself a lot of unnecessary pain. If you want to play it smart—if you muster the courage to surrender; if you take your broken pieces to the foot of the cross—you'll discover a new world of possibility.

Phase 3: The Catalyst Phase

A catalyst is something that stimulates or precipitates a reaction, development, or change. It rouses the mind or spirit or incites to activity. Other words for catalyst include: stimulus, impetus, incentive, motivation, spur, stimulant, boost, encouragement, inducement, or invitation. When you allow God to help you move into the catalyst phase, you'll know you're breaking free and moving on.

As George Matheson wrote:

There are songs which can only be learned in the valley. No art can teach them; no rules of voice can make them perfectly sung. Their music is in the heart. They are songs of memory, of personal experience. They bring out their burden from the shadow of the past; they mount on the wings of yesterday. . . .

The Father is training thee for the part the angels cannot sing; and the school is sorrow. I have heard many say that He sends sorrow to prove thee; may He send sorrow to educate thee, to train thee for the choir invisible.[9]

Most people have never thought much about the value of failure. Maybe that's because our culture is so focused on ambition and success. As I researched this book, I discovered that most self-help and inspirational books tell you how to succeed, not how to learn from failure. Yet John Bunyan wrote in his spiritual autobiography, *Grace Abounding,* "I never saw those heights and depths in grace, and love, and mercy, as I saw after this temptation: great sins draw out great grace; and where guilt is most terrible and fierce, there the mercy of God in Christ, when showed to the soul, appears most high and mighty."[10]

When we fail, we have the opportunity to discover certain truths about ourselves that might otherwise have remained hidden and out of reach. One of the advantages of being thrown back to the basics is that we're reminded that there are basics to fall back on. I believe it was Andre Crouch who wrote, "If I'd never had a problem, I'd have never known that God could solve them; I'd never know what faith in His Word could do."

Small Beginnings

1. In your own words, write a one-sentence definition for each of the fight, flight, and faith responses.

   fight response:

   flight response:

   faith response:

2. Think back to a recent failure in your life. What were some of the physical, mental, emotional, or spiritual warning signs that you experienced?

3. What's one insight God has given you in this chapter that you can apply the next time you see one of those warning signs?

4. God's View of Failure

'd like to ask you to do something that may sound a bit weird. If you're reading this book in a public place, people may wonder what you're doing, but that's okay. Enjoy watching the puzzled looks on their faces as they try to pretend they're not watching you.

Take this book in your right hand and hold it in front of your face at arm's length. What do you see? The answer is obvious. You see the room you're sitting in with a book in front of your face at arm's length. How much of your view is blocked by the book? Probably not much.

Now take the book and hold it halfway between arm's length and your face. What do you see? That's right. You see more of the book and less of the room. The size of the book hasn't changed, but bringing it a short distance closer to your face has affected your view.

Next, hold the book right in front of your eyes, and look straight ahead. What do you see? The cover of the book and some light coming from around the edges. Has the size of the book changed? Of course not. But now it has blocked out your entire view of the room. It has become the only thing you see.

One of the most beautiful and majestic sights in the world is the range of mountains known as the Grand Tetons. If you were to go to the base of the Tetons and hold this book in front of your face, what would you see? That's right, you would see the same thing you saw a few minutes ago: a close-up view of the book cover.

I've asked you to do this silly little exercise because it illustrates a powerful spiritual principle, one that can have an enormous influence on the degree to which you're able to experience victory over failure and grow to enjoy the abundant Christian life. When failure comes our way (or any other kind of problem, for that matter), it's our nature to focus on it. The more we dwell on the setback, the closer we get to it, the more we look at it in exclusion to other things, the bigger it *appears* to be.

To a great degree, our perspective on our failures will determine how they affect our lives. When we try to face our difficulties with our own wisdom and in our own strength, we're likely to spend much of our time staring in the face of failure and overwhelmed with feelings of discouragement, depression, and defeat.

If, on the other hand, we choose to look at our failures from God's point of view, things will be different. Yes, we'll still get down. We'll still experience discouragement. But we won't be crushed. We won't have to stay stuck in the rut of reinventing the wheel, of making the same mistakes over and over. We'll know what it's like to become people who are "more than conquerors."

As I sat down to write out my initial thoughts for this book, I realized I had never done a thorough study of what God thinks and says about failure. I knew how I and my teachers and our society viewed failure, but what about God's view? When all is said and done, that's the most important perspective, isn't it? Every day, every situation, every success, and every setback must be looked at through His eyes. So I did an exhaustive word study of *failure, success,* and related terms. I looked at every biblical passage that mentioned them, and I did numerous studies of the lives of Old and New Testament characters.

From Genesis to Revelation, the Bible talks about the failure of mankind and the faithfulness of God. The life of David and the Book of Psalms proved to be gold mines of understanding. David spent much of his life riding a roller coaster from the highs of success to the lows of failure and back up to success.

In my search of God's view of failure, I discovered six key principles: God knows we'll fail; He allows us to fail; He's with us when we fail, and if our failure involves sin He is ready to forgive; He sees beyond our failure; He understands the potential value of our failure; and He can use our failures for good. Let's take a closer look at each of these.

1. God Knows We'll Fail

Have you ever thought about the fact that God is never surprised? Even when we blow it, He isn't surprised. Disappointed? Yes! Surprised? No. There are times when even I have been surprised by my blind spots and weaknesses, but God wasn't.

David had a unique relationship with God. He experienced the power of God's hand on his life and enjoyed an incredible intimacy with God. He saw God take him from being a simple sheep herder to being a national hero when he killed Goliath and later becoming the wealthy and powerful king of his nation. Yet David also knew the dark depths of failure. Read what he had to say in Psalm 103:

The Lord is compassionate and gracious, slow to anger, abounding in love. He will not always accuse, nor will He harbor His anger forever; He does not treat us as our sins deserve or repay us according to our iniquities. For as high as the heavens are above the earth, so great is His love for those who fear Him; as far as the east is from the west, so far has He removed our transgressions from us. As a father has compassion on his children, so the Lord has compassion on those who fear Him; for He knows how we are formed, He remembers that we are dust. As for a man, his days are like grass, he flourishes like a flower of the field; the wind blows over it and it is gone, and its place remembers it no more. But from everlasting to everlasting the Lord's love is with those who fear Him and His righteousness with their children's children — with those who keep His covenant and remember to obey His precepts (Ps. 103:8-18).

Here we see a God who knows the frailty and weakness of people, but who loves us anyway. We find a similar thought in Hebrews 4:15: "For we do not have a high priest who is unable to sympathize with our weaknesses, but we have one who has been tempted in every way, just as we are — yet was without sin."

First John is one of the most encouraging books in all of Scripture. In the first verse of 1 John 2, John wrote, "My dear children, I write this to you so that you will not sin." He was saying that God's will for us is that we don't sin. We're to do all we can to avoid it. If the text stopped there, it would be rather discouraging. But it doesn't.

He continued, "But if anybody does sin, we have one who speaks to the Father in our defense — Jesus Christ, the Righteous One. He is the atoning sacrifice for our sins, and not only for ours but also for the sins of the whole world" (1 John 2:1-2). It's as if God is saying through John, "Whatever you do, don't sin." But since He knows how we're made and the effects of sin on our lives, He adds, "But when you do sin, I want you to remember where to look, who to turn to, and what to do."

God knows we're frail. He understands the effects sin has had on our lives. He also understands that we're in a battle, that "our struggle is not against flesh and blood, but against the rulers, against the authorities, against the powers of this dark world and against the spiritual forces of evil in the heavenly realms" (Eph. 6:12). He knows that Satan spends night and day seeking ways to trick, trip, and trap us.

I've talked with many Christians who view one evidence of maturity and success in the Christian life as the lack of struggle. But in reality, our struggles are an indication that something is happening in our lives, and they're a key part of the process of becoming Christlike men and women. Our failure may make us feel unworthy, but God will never make us feel worthless.

2. He Allows Us to Fail

Not only does God know we'll fail, but He also *allows* us to fail. One of my favorite benedictions is found in Jude 24: "Now to Him who is able to keep you without stumbling, or slipping, or falling and to present [you] unblemished (blameless and faultless) before the presence of His glory — with unspeakable, ecstatic delight — in triumphant joy and exultation" (AMP).

Did you notice the first part of that verse? Jude made it clear that God is able to keep us from slipping, tripping, stumbling, or falling. Yet He often chooses not to exercise that power and to let us fail instead.

The farther I walk along the pathway of parenting, the better I understand God's role as my Heavenly Father and the ways in which He parents me. One of the best ways we learn is through experience, and the kinds of experience that prove to be our best teachers tend to be the painful ones. I have three sons, and all of them love to swim. However, the process of teaching them took some time. The first step was to teach them respect for the water.

From the time he was able to walk, my youngest son, Andrew, loved to go to the pool. He had great confidence in the baby pool and couldn't understand why we wouldn't let him jump in the big pool with his brothers. No matter how hard we tried to explain it to him, he didn't get it.

One day we were changing clothes in the locker room, getting ready to go to the pool, and Andrew went out of the locker room ahead of me. He thought he had lost me and was finally free to do whatever he wanted. So what did he do? You guessed it; he immediately headed for the big pool and jumped in. When he came up for air, he had a panicked look on his face. As he gasped for breath, he saw my face and tried to call out my name. In the process, he took in a mouthful of water, and down he went.

I immediately jumped into the water, pulled him to the surface, and held him next to me. I didn't scold him, yell at him, or try to shame him. When he calmed down, I sat him on the side of the pool and calmly asked, "Was that fun?"

His immediate response was an emphatic "No!"

I continued, "Would you like to do that again?"

I could tell by the look on his face that he was insulted that I would ask such a ridiculous question. He didn't even answer me. Instead, he stood up, went over to the baby pool, and avoided the big pool from then on.

During my life, I've had many failures. Some of the most valuable research for this book came out of the laboratory of my own life. Some of my failures grew out of selfishness, immaturity, or stupidity, but the most painful ones came from disobeying my Heavenly Father.

God didn't cause my failures, yet He *did* allow them. But He never allowed me to experience more than I could handle. Just as I reached out to Andrew in the pool, God has continued to reach out to me. He has drawn me closer to Himself, and more times than I can count, He has pulled me out of quicksand and put my feet on dry, solid ground. He has promised to do that for all His children, including you.

3. He Is with Us When We Fail, and If Our Failure Involves Sin, He's Ready to Forgive

Our failures force to the surface our deepest understandings (and at times *mis*understandings) of God. That's one of the many ways He uses our weaknesses and setbacks. Failures force us to toss aside the clothing of our past successes and accomplishments. When we're stripped naked and laid bare before

God, we're able to see His face and hear His voice with the greatest clarity. Often at such times, when the purifying fire burns the hottest, we have the best potential for the kinds of growth that lead to true maturity.

When things are going well, it's easy to proclaim our belief in a merciful, gracious, forgiving, and loving God. But when failure dumps us in the trenches of spiritual warfare, some of us discover that our view of God is actually one of a merciless taskmaster or a critical and punitive parent. But as Nehemiah 9:17 tells us, He is "a forgiving God, gracious and compassionate, slow to anger and abounding in love." Not only does God expect us to fail and allow it to happen, but He's with us when it does. Look at what David wrote: "If the Lord delights in a man's way, He makes his steps firm; though he stumble, he will not fall, for the Lord upholds him with His hand. I was young and now I am old, yet I have never seen the righteous forsaken or their children begging bread" (Ps. 37:23-25). And consider this:

> The Lord is close to the brokenhearted
> and saves those who are crushed in spirit (Ps. 34:18).
> The sacrifices of God are a broken spirit;
> a broken and contrite heart, O God, you will not despise
> (Ps. 51:17).
> The Lord upholds all those who fall
> and lifts up all who are bowed down. . . .
> The Lord is near to all who call on him,
> to all who call on Him in truth.
> He fulfills the desires of those who fear Him;
> He hears their cry and saves them (Ps. 145:14, 18-19).

The God who has promised to never leave us or forsake us is the same God who is ready and able to forgive. In Psalm 103:3, we find a God "who forgives all your sins." And in Isaiah 30:18, we're told, "The Lord longs to be gracious to you; He rises to show you compassion. For the Lord is a God of justice. Blessed are all who wait for Him."

I wholeheartedly agree with Erwin Lutzer that the greatest mistake Christians make is not our failure when trying to live for Christ. Rather, it's that we don't understand God's provision for sin, defeat, and guilt![1] We seem to have limited understanding of what took place at the cross. We're shocked when we fail. Then we become preoccupied with our failure. We try to create some kind of righteousness to "pay" for our sin, forgetting that His grace is greater than all our sin.

Let's be clear. Disobedience to God is a very serious thing. God abhors sin. Our sin caused the death of His only begotten Son. Yet God can use our sin to drive us to the cross, where we experience forgiveness, renew our perspective, and receive the grace to move on . . . perhaps a bit sadder but much wiser.

Some of the "greats" of the Christian faith were broken by sin and disobedience, yet God didn't dump them in the rubbish heap. Adam and Eve blew it. Moses made mistakes; his murder of the Egyptian cost him forty years in the wilderness. Abraham started strong, but once he got into Egypt, he blew it. David's sin of adultery and murder cost him his integrity and the life of his son. Elijah allowed his depression to get so far out of control that he begged God to take his life. Jonah's failure caused him to reject God's clearly revealed plan. But God gave every one of them a second chance.

Max Lucado has given us a remarkable description of God's forgiveness:

It was like discovering the prize in a box of Cracker Jacks or spotting a little pearl in a box of buttons or stumbling across a ten dollar bill in a drawer full of envelopes.

It was small enough to overlook. Only two words. I know I'd read that passage a hundred times. But I'd never seen it. Maybe I'd passed over it in the excitement of the resurrection. Or, since Mark's account of the resurrection is by far the briefest of the four, maybe I'd just not paid too much attention. . . .

But I won't miss it again. It's highlighted in yellow and

underlined in red. You might want to do the same. Look in Mark, chapter 16. Read the first five verses about the women's surprise when they find the stone moved to the side. . . . Go a bit further. Get your pencil ready and enjoy this jewel in the seventh verse. . . . "But go, tell his disciples and Peter that he is going before you to Galilee."

Did you see it? Read it again. (This time I italicized the words.)

"But go, tell his disciples *and Peter* that he is going before you to Galilee."

Now tell me if that's not a hidden treasure.

If I might paraphrase the words, "Don't stay here, go tell the disciples," a pause, then a smile, "and *especially* tell Peter that he is going before you to Galilee."

What a line. It's as if all of heaven had watched Peter fall — and it's as if all of heaven wanted to help him back up again. "Be sure and tell Peter that he's not left out. Tell him that one failure doesn't make a flop."

Whew!

No wonder they call it the gospel of the second chance.

Not many second chances exist in the world today. Just ask the kid who didn't make the little league team or the fellow who got the pink slip or the mother of three who got dumped for a "pretty little thing."

Not many second chances. Nowadays it's more like, "It's now or never." "Around here we don't tolerate incompetence." "It's a dog-eat-dog world."

Jesus has a simple answer to our masochistic mania. "It's a dog-eat-dog world?" he would say. "Then don't live with the dogs." That makes sense doesn't it? Why let a bunch of other failures tell you how much of a failure you are?

Sure you can have a second chance.

Just ask Peter. One minute he felt lower than a snake's belly and the next minute he was the high hog at the trough. Even the angels wanted this distraught netcaster to know that it wasn't over. The message came loud and clear from the celestial Throne Room through the divine courier. "Be sure and tell Peter that he gets to bat again. . . ."

It's not every day that you get a second chance. Peter must have known that. The next time he saw Jesus, he got so excited that he barely got his britches on before he jumped into the cold water of the Sea of Galilee. It was also enough, so they say, to cause this backwoods Galilean to carry the gospel of the second chance all the way to Rome where they killed him. If you've ever wondered what would cause a man to be willing to be crucified upside down, maybe now you know.

It's not every day that you find someone who will give you a second chance—much less someone who will give you a second chance every day.

But in Jesus, Peter found both.[2]

4. He Understands the Potential Value of Our Failure

It's more than enough that we've been forgiven. But God doesn't stop there. He delights in doing "immeasurably more than all we ask or imagine" (Eph. 3:20). And that includes using our failures in a constructive way for our growth.

Most people want to repress, deny, and ignore their mistakes. But that's not God's perspective. He knows that in every failure lie seeds of growth and that apart from failure, we would have little need for His forgiveness, His communion, or His help. He doesn't like failure, but He knows that in His hands, it can be one of our greatest teachers.

In Augustine's *Confessions*, he wrote:

What is it, therefore, that goes on within the soul, since it takes greater delight if things that it loves are found or restored to it than if it had always possessed them? Other things bear witness to this, and all are filled with proofs that cry aloud, "Thus it is!" The victorious general holds his triumph: yet unless he had fought, he would never have won the victory, and the greater was the danger in battle, the greater is the joy in the triumph. The storm tosses seafarers about, and threatens them with shipwreck; they all grow pale at their coming death. Then the sky and the sea become calm and they exult exceedingly, just as they had feared exceedingly. A dear friend is ill, and his pulse tells us of his bad case. All those who long to see him in good health are in mind sick along with him. He gets well again, and although he does not yet walk with his former vigor, there is joy such as did not obtain before when he walked well and strong.

Everywhere a greater joy is preceded by a greater suffering.[3]

I can't fully express how wonderful it is for me to know that I don't need to pretend—not with God, not with my family, and not with my friends. If perfection were the goal, God could accomplish that purpose much easier without us. God *is* perfection, and we *do* fail.

But instant perfection isn't God's purpose for you and me. As I've studied God's Word, I've discovered that He allows us to participate in life much as I allow one of my sons to help with a project around the house. It's almost a given that I could do the job better and faster than my son, but the ultimate goal of our relationship isn't doing something "better" and "faster." It has much to do with the building of our relationship, the modeling of Christian values, and the realization of worth.

It's interesting to note that many in the business world are starting to realize what God has known since the beginning of time. As early as 1978, a book was published in the field of organizational development that dealt with the value of failures. Toward the beginning, the authors wrote that in universities, consulting firms, and organizations leaders hide their failures and advertise their successes. This leaves the public with an unrealistic, inflated, and distorted perspective on organization development. It also denies individuals the opportunity to benefit from their own and the mistakes of others.[4]

More recently, Vic Sussman, in an article entitled "To Win, First You Must Lose," asked:

> Do you ever wonder why success keeps dancing just be-yond your acquisitive fingertips? A chorus of business gu-rus has the answer. Success eludes you — ready for this? — because you haven't failed enough.
>
> A dozen win-it-all books tout failure as the castor oil of success. The idea isn't that you're supposed to fling your-self into certain disaster because you will be mystically rewarded with triumph. Rather, it's a simple recognition that people who willingly risk failure and learn from the pain of loss have the best chance of succeeding at whatever they try.[5]

In a televised interview, Ross Perot stated, "Continuous suc-cess builds arrogance and complacency." He went on to say that we should simply brush failure aside and look at it as the cost of seeking new challenges: "I want people who love the battlefield, people willing to go to the wall." Perot said that unsuccessful companies reflexively avoid risks even when a smart gamble might pay off. "I've never known an honest mistake that really hurt the business," Perot said. "You learn a great deal more from what doesn't work than from what works routinely."

5. He Sees Beyond Our Failure

Because God understands the potential value of our failure, He's able to see beyond it. That's not so easy for us. So often our first response is to focus on the failure and panic: "My ministry is over." "God will never be able to use me again." "My kids will be damaged for life." We develop myopic blinders for the here and now.

Don't get me wrong. We need to have a here-and-now focus. We do need to think and pray about how to cope. But unless we allow God to help us put this piece of our lives in the bigger picture, it's probably not going to make much sense. We'll be reduced to surviving rather than growing.

Take a look at Hebrews 11. That's the well-known "Faith Hall of Fame" chapter. It gives a long list of ordinary men and women who allowed God to use them to accomplish extraordinary things: ". . . who by faith conquered kingdoms, performed acts of righteousness, obtained promises, shut the mouths of lions, quenched the power of fire, escaped the edge of the sword, from weakness were made strong . . . put foreign armies to flight" (vv. 33-34, NASB).

That sounds pretty exciting until you read what they had to endure: "They were stoned, they were sawn in two, they were tempted, they were put to death with the sword; they went about in sheepskins, in goatskins, being destitute, afflicted, ill-treated (men of whom the world was not worthy), wandering in deserts and mountains and caves and holes in the ground" (vv. 37-38, NASB).

Their success didn't just happen. They weren't some superior breed of people who didn't make mistakes. In fact, there are a lot of failures in the "Faith Hall of Fame." Noah struggled with alcohol abuse and immorality. Abraham struggled with lying and taking things into his own hands. Sarah doubted God and was selfish and cruel to Hagar. Jacob was a liar and cheated his brother, Esau. Moses started by killing a man and never fully learned to control his anger. Rahab was a prostitute. Samson turned his back on God and lost his sight and his ministry. David was guilty of adultery and murder. Samuel had great faith but was an abysmal failure as a father.

And yet in every case, God didn't toss them out when they blew it. He was able to see beyond their failure. If you go back to verse 34, it says that "from weakness [they] were made strong." They became men and women "of whom the world was not worthy" (v. 38). Wow! Let me say it again. *Wow!* Even if you've been a murderer, an adulterer, alcoholic, liar, or prostitute, God can still use you.

Obviously, personal failure isn't a requirement for success. But our failures can be used as stepping stones to a deeper relationship with God because of the incredible generosity of His forgiveness and acceptance. His grace not only covers our failures, it also transforms them.

Romans 8:28, which says "that in all things God works for the good of those who love Him," doesn't mean that everything that happens to us is good. It means that God can cause all those things to work together for good. That includes the trials Paul mentioned in verses 35 and 36. The amazing thing is that Paul didn't say *some* things, *many* things, or *most* things. He said God can cause *all* things to work together for good.

In the last two verses of Romans 8, Paul listed ten things that can't separate us from God's love. But an unbiblical view of failure can cause us to "feel" as if we've been separated from Him. Even though it can't be true and will never be true, the fact that it "feels" true can cause our discouragement to sink into a deep depression.

But this is the God of Hebrews 11, the God who can take broken pieces and make a useful vessel, who delights in blessing His people, who wants to do immeasurably more than all we ask or imagine, who is committed to helping us become more than conquerors.

In God's hand, failure can refine and teach us in ways that success can't. Failure reaches down into the depth of who we are and exposes deep-seated pockets of selfishness and pride. It makes us aware of our limitations. It increases our sensitivity to others. It humbles us. It helps us understand the high calling of being a servant. It reminds us how important it is to "set [our] minds on things above, not on earthly things" (Col. 3:2). It increases our confidence that "He who began a good work in you will carry it on to completion until the day of Christ Jesus" (Phil. 1:6).

Small Beginnings

1. Think of a time when God brought something good out of something bad in your life. What happened? How does that make you feel about His ability to bring good out of your future failures?

2. Do you have trouble believing God still loves you and has a purpose for you even though He knows you'll fail? Why or why not?

3. If you could ask God a question about your most recent failure, what would it be?

4. What one thing you've learned in this chapter sticks out in your mind as something you'll want to remember the next time you fail?

5. Getting through Failure
Part 1

The call was like so many others I've received. I could tell from the shakiness in her voice that Mary was in a crisis. "I've put off calling you for several months," she said. "I thought that things would clear up and I would start to feel better. But they haven't cleared up, and I don't feel better."

Mary's first response to the events in her life was to get angry. For a while, the energy from that powerful emotion carried her through. But when her anger subsided and she was able to see more clearly, she felt overwhelmed by emotions she didn't understand and wasn't sure how to deal with.

As she told her story, it became clear that her crisis wasn't due to any one thing. It was the cumulative effect of many small things she could have handled one by one. But when she was forced to face them together, it became overwhelming.

Mary had been divorced several years earlier. The divorce had been messy, and her ex-husband seemed to enjoy making things as difficult as possible for her. She had a good relationship with her children, but her oldest son had started running with a rough group at college, and she carried a lot of concern for him.

Her company had been taken over by a larger corporation. She didn't lose her job, but she had been demoted and had her pay cut.

She had recently broken up with a fine man who wasn't a Christian. She had allowed herself to become emotionally and then physically involved, and she was struggling with guilt over her sin and grief over the loss.

In the middle of our first session, she blurted out, "I was a failure as a wife. I'm a failure as a mom, I'm a failure as an employee, and I'm a failure as a Christian." Through the tears she continued, "It seems like the harder I try, the worse things get." Looking down at the floor, she slowly and quietly said, "I don't know what to do. I don't know where to start. And I don't really know if I even care."

After a brief pause, I looked her in the eyes and said, "Mary, I believe you do care. If you didn't, you wouldn't have called me, and you wouldn't be sitting here right now." She looked up and responded with a faint smile that let me know she had heard me. I continued, "And what's even more important is that God not only cares, but He wants to meet you in your failure, help you to learn from it, and take you into an even deeper love relationship with Him."

I went on to explain some of the principles I've already presented in previous chapters. Mary was especially surprised when I opened the Bible and talked to her about God's view of failure. But Mary was in crisis. She didn't need me to quote Bible verses. She needed to understand how those verses could be applied to where she was right now. She also needed a specific plan to help her get unstuck and get on with her life. In this chapter and the next, I want to give you the same effective process I gave Mary.

Do you remember the last time you made a major mistake or experienced a significant setback? When was it? What did it feel like? Were the painful emotions more intense than usual? Did they last longer than usual? What was your immediate response? Did it help? How did your friends respond?

Sometimes the pain of a failure hits us head-on. But at other times, it sort of sneaks up behind us, catches one of our feet just as we're getting ready to take another step, and suddenly we find ourselves flat on our face. We're in a crisis and don't know what to do.

Given our cultural taboo against failure, it seems the only time most people begin to think about it is when they're in the middle of it. Unfortunately, that's the worst time to start to deal with it. Your energy is depleted, your perspective is distorted, and you're more prone to negative thinking.

When the pain hits, our natural response is to seek relief. When we feel bad, we want to feel good again. Our immediate reaction is to rush through the experience as quickly as possible to get "feeling good" again—to get back to "normal." In this context, "normal" usually means not having to be aware of our weaknesses or shortcomings. It usually means being able to go back to the illusion that "I'm okay; you're okay; everything's okay."

In the short term, we can wade through the setbacks of life in ways that help us *get* through but don't allow us to *grow* through them. We've learned how to react but not how to respond. But with each repetition, the weeds get a little thicker and the water gets a little deeper.

In the long term, this is a guaranteed recipe for disaster. This "feel good quick" scheme actually sets us up for greater failure down the road. Unfortunately, we can't see that coming. But when it does, we're faced with an even larger, more complex problem. And suddenly we realize we haven't got the resources or strength to deal with it.

Strength and character aren't found; they're forged in the furnace of failure. Over the years, I've developed a plan for growing through the difficult times. This isn't theory. It's based on the clear teaching of God's Word and has been proved in the crucible of my own life and the lives of many hundreds of men and women I've counseled. The twelve steps I'm suggesting are simple but not easy. They do, however, *work*. I'll list them first and then develop each in more detail.

1. **Acknowledge** God's presence.
2. **Adopt** an attitude of praise.

3. **Ask** God for His guidance.
4. **Align** your perspectives to His.
5. **Acknowledge** the anatomy of failure.
6. **Admit** you made a mistake.
7. **Accept** responsibility for it.
8. **Analyze** what happened.
9. **Assess** what you could do differently next time.
10. **Accept** God's forgiveness.
11. **Activate** your plan.
12. **Announce** what God has taught you.

Step 1: Acknowledge God's Presence

Why do some people consistently crumble under the effects of failure while others seem energized by them? Why do some seem to wilt and fade away while others gain backbone, character, and conviction through the process? Why do honesty and transparency seem to come so easily for some while others are scared to death and afraid to trust, unwilling to risk exposure?

It's not because of some magic character strength that was genetically encoded. It's not because God loves some more than others. It's not because others' lives have been easier than yours. It's because those who do better have learned the simple secret of where to turn in times of trouble.

This first step is simple. It doesn't take much time. But it can determine the outcome of your present situation. Mary had been so focused on her problems that she didn't see God's provisions. She was so discouraged by what she had done wrong that she didn't even notice how God was honoring what she was doing right. She was so absorbed by the temporal that she had totally lost sight of the eternal.

When I fail, the thing I'm least likely to do is to acknowledge God's presence. Usually I'm not even aware of His presence. But I'm acutely aware of my pain, of people who might be affected by my failure, and of others who might learn about my failure and think less of me as a result. All those thoughts flood my consciousness and, like a runaway train, can push me to the brink of panic.

In St. Louis, there's a large switchyard through which pass most of the trains that go to that great city. In that switchyard is a yard house that controls all the train traffic. In that yard house is one small switch that begins with just a thin piece of steel but eventually moves heavy steel tracks to direct a train away from the one main track and onto another. If the yardmaster flicks that switch one way, the train will end up in San Francisco. If he moves the switch the other way, that same train will eventually arrive in New York. San Francisco or New York? The difference is determined by the simple flick of a finger.

This first step of acknowledging God's presence is a lot like that switch. The small and simple choice of what we choose to focus on as we're feeling drained and discouraged can lead to two dramatically different destinations. When events have carried you into rapids that are beyond your control; when your dreams of success or desire for emotional survival have gone haywire; when your great expectations have blown up in your face; when life doesn't seem anything even close to fair, *don't even think of turning away from Him.* Don't run and hide. After all, when has that ever really helped? Turn *to* Him.

The times when you least feel His presence, when it seems He moved and didn't leave a forwarding address, are often the times when He wants to do a major work in your life. In his classic book *The Screwtape Letters,* C.S. Lewis presented a series of letters from a senior tempter, Screwtape, to his young nephew, Wormwood. Wormwood had been given the seemingly simple task of tempting a human soul to hell. All Wormwood had to do was keep the person from becoming a Christian. Unfortunately (for Wormwood), he blew it and allowed his person to become a believer.

But all was not lost, Screwtape told him. It was still possible to keep this human being from learning, growing, and experiencing the abundant and victorious Christian life. Uncle Screwtape offered his fiendishly clever advice on the most effective ways the devil uses to defeat and discourage young Christians. In the course of this correspondence, Lewis also explained some of the key ways God uses to help us learn and grow.

One of the most powerful principles is found in letter eight. There Lewis described an experience of emotional and spiritual highs and lows that is common to all of us. Screwtape taught Wormwood about what he called the "Law of Undulation." He said that the process of undulation is one of the best tools God uses to help Christians mature, that down times, or "troughs," are a normal part of the human life.

Think about it. At times we experience an energy, joy, and emotional richness in our walk with God. We're dramatically aware of His power and presence. At those times we feel faith and strength. We ask God for mountains to climb. But there are other times when we struggle with discouragement, depression, and failure. These periods of dryness and dullness can produce a numbness and a sense of spiritual poverty. No matter how hard we try, we can't find God anywhere. Our prayers seem to bounce off the ceiling. It's as if He has deserted us.

During those low times, we feel particularly weak and vulnerable, and the evil one has an excellent opportunity for temptation. But as Screwtape warned Wormwood, God allows those dips. He withdraws Himself from our conscious experience to give us the opportunity to strengthen our ability to *choose* to trust and obey Him. Not because we feel like it; it may be the last thing we feel like doing. But it's easy to obey God, to set our minds on things above, when we feel strong and things are going great. It takes a whole different level of maturity to obey Him when He doesn't seem to be there.

"It is during such trough periods, much more than during the peak periods, that it [the Christian] is growing into the sort of creature he [God] wants it to be,"[1] Screwtape told Wormwood. And the prayers people offer in this state of spiritual dryness are the ones that please God best. If Christians choose to learn and grow, He's even pleased with their stumbles.

Screwtape continued, "Do not be deceived, Wormwood. Our

cause is never more in danger than when a human, no longer desiring, but still intending, to do our enemy's will, looks round upon a universe from which every trace of him [God] seems to have vanished, and asks why he has been forsaken, and still obeys."[2]

Those who have learned the secrets of faith that come only through failure also understand the words of King Solomon: "My son, if you accept my words and store up my commands within you, turning your ear to wisdom and applying your heart to understanding, and if you call out for insight and cry aloud for understanding, and if you look for it as for silver and search for it as for hidden treasure, then you will understand the fear of the Lord and find the knowledge of God. For the Lord gives wisdom, and from His mouth come knowledge and understanding" (Prov. 2:1-6).

Step 2: Adopt an Attitude of Praise

I know what you're saying to yourself after reading the heading above: "C'mon, Oliver, get real. When I'm feeling down and out, the last thing I want to do is praise the Lord." Hey, that's okay. Others have told me the same thing. In fact, when I was just starting to learn this principle, there were times when I told the Lord that myself.

William Law, a sixteenth-century clergyman, said, "If anyone could tell you the shortest, surest way to all happiness and perfection, he must tell you to make it a rule to yourself to thank and praise God for everything that happens to you. For it is certain that whatever seeming calamity happens to you, if you thank and praise God in it, you turn it into a blessing."

When we look at life through the eyes of our own weaknesses and imperfections, we have what I call a "failure focus." But when we choose to look at life through the eyes of who God is, what Christ accomplished for us on the cross, the many promises God has given us, and what He has already accomplished in our lives and praise Him for those things, we're able to move from a failure focus to a faith focus. And that change makes all the difference in the world.

In 1 Thessalonians 5:18, the Bible tells us to give thanks *in* all things. We may not be able to give thanks *for* all things, but in every situation we can praise God for His character, His faithfulness, and His promises. Whenever I personally struggle with this small, simple, and yet essential second step, I'm reminded of a story that Corrie ten Boom told.

In *The Hiding Place,* she related an incident that taught her always to be thankful. She and her sister, Betsie, had just been transferred to the worst German prison camp they had seen, Ravensbruck. On entering the barracks, they found them extremely overcrowded and flea-infested.

That morning, their Scripture reading in 1 Thessalonians had reminded them to rejoice always, pray constantly, and give thanks in all circumstances. Betsie told Corrie to stop and thank the Lord for every detail of their new living quarters. Corrie flatly refused to give thanks for the fleas, but Betsie persisted, and Corrie finally succumbed to her pleadings.

During their time at that camp, they were surprised to find how openly they could hold Bible study and prayer meetings without guard interference. It wasn't until several months later that they learned the guards would not enter the barracks because of the fleas!

Corrie started by *in* all things giving thanks. And because Romans 8:28 is true — because God can cause all things to work together for good — she discovered the power of praise.

Jack Hayford has written that when we praise God:

a day or a circumstance is moved out of the fog of limited potential into the realm of heaven's promised purpose. Praise clears your head in the atmosphere of God's throne where one kneels. It sharpens your vision to see through the eyes of God; and it expands your soul beyond the smallness of purpose when the focus is only on self-centered concerns.

Praise opens the heart to the receptivity of God's truth. Praise humbles the soul and restores child-likeness. Praise peels back pride and rips away the flesh's tendency to posture itself. We find reality on our knees. God is touched by upraised hands. Wisdom and understanding flow back into lips which first utter thanks to the Most High.[3]

Almost every day, an essential part of my morning ritual is to spend some time in the Word, in a Bible commentary or devotional book, and in prayer. I always begin my prayer by praising God. Praise provides the perspective that helps me look at my day through God's eyes. If I'm in the midst of a particularly difficult time, praise helps me get through it. As I thank God for His person, His promises, His provisions, and His power, I realize I'm not alone. He hasn't deserted me. He will help me get through it. And more than that, He will help me be stronger because of it.

I once heard a creative story told of a day when the sun didn't rise. Six A.M. came, and there was no sign of dawn. At 7 A.M., there was still no ray of light. At noon, it was black as midnight. No birds sang, and only the hoot of an owl broke the silence. After the long, dark afternoon hours came evening. But no one slept that night.

Some wept; some wrung their hands in despair. Every church was filled with people on their knees. And they stayed there the entire night. At the end of that long night of agony, millions of eager, tear-streaked faces were turned toward the east. When the sky began to grow red and the sun rose, there was a loud shout of joy. Millions of lips said, "Praise the Lord!" because the sun had risen after one day of darkness.

The darkness of failure can sometimes dull us to the consistency of God's many blessings. The greatest thing about the mercies of God is that they're new and fresh every morning and every evening. Remember, even in the midst of darkness, to give thanks. There's a song that clearly and simply explains the importance of this step.

"Praise the Lord"

When you're up against a struggle that shatters all your
dreams,
When your hopes have been cruelly crushed by Satan's
manifested schemes,
When you feel the urge within you to submit to earthly
fear,
Don't let the faith you're standing in seem to disappear.
Now Satan is a liar and he wants to make us think that we
are paupers,
But we know quite well we're children of the King.
So lift up your mighty shield of faith for the battle must be
won,
We know that Jesus Christ is risen so His work on earth is
done.
Praise the Lord, He can work through those who praise
Him
Praise the Lord, for our God inhabits praise
Praise the Lord, for the chains that seem to bind you
Serve only to remind you that they drop powerless behind
you
When you praise Him.[4]

When Mary, the woman I mentioned at the beginning of this
chapter, took the time to thank God, she was amazed to discover how her spirits were lifted. Her problems didn't magically
disappear. "But I left that time of prayer and praise with a sense
of His presence and power and a new perspective," she said. "I
left with a clear sense of hope and anticipation for how God was
going to continue the work He had begun."

Step 3: Ask God for His Guidance

Jeremiah understood what it meant to have a bad day. He had
many of them. He understood pain, discouragement, frustra-

tion, and failure. He was called the "weeping prophet." In Jeremiah 33, God gave him a promise that is as potent today as it was then. Call to Me, He said, and . . .

I will answer you.

I will tell you great and unsearchable things you do not know.

I will bring health and healing.

I will let the people enjoy abundant peace and security.

I will restore your fortunes.

I will rebuild them.

I will cleanse them from all their iniquity.

I will pardon their iniquities (3:3-8).

When we haven't cultivated the ability to learn from small failures, it may take a first-rate failure—one we can't deny, overlook, or repackage into "one of God's little blessings in disguise" or "a cloud with a silver lining"—to get our attention. And then the real courage comes when we choose to jump into the experience, ask God for His guidance, and listen to Him long enough to learn something.

As a young Christian, my immediate response to failure was never one of looking for God's face, listening for His voice, or lingering for His touch. I always looked for Him in the obvious places—in the Bible, at a praise service, at prayer meetings, or in church. I never dreamed He would meet me in my failures. I thought that if I worked harder, learned more, earned more, and denied myself more, I would be more successful as a Christian.

We look for God in the dynamic and dramatic—in a dream, a vision, or a special "word of knowledge." Sometimes He speaks to us in those ways. But more often than not, He speaks to us in the still, small voice of His Spirit.

At one point in the story of Elijah, he had just seen God use him to call down fire from heaven, consume an altar that had been drenched with buckets of water, and destroy 450 prophets of Baal. He should have been on a ticker-tape victory parade, but instead he had signed up as a pallbearer for his own funeral. In a matter of hours, he had gone from the mountaintop to a spiritual death valley. His change of perspective took him from a faith focus to a fear focus. He heard that wicked Queen Jezebel was after him, so he ran for his life. Rather than focusing on what he knew God *could* do, he focused on what Jezebel *might* do. That shift in viewpoint produced a profound shift in his perception.

The mighty Prophet Elijah ended up sitting under a juniper tree asking God to take his life. "Nobody loves me. Everybody hates me. I've had enough. I can't take it anymore." From the juniper tree, he spent the night hiding in a cave. We pick up the story in 1 Kings 19:9:

> And the word of the Lord came to him: "What are you doing here, Elijah?"
>
> He replied, "I have been very zealous for the Lord God Almighty. The Israelites have rejected Your covenant, broken down Your altars, and put Your prophets to death with the sword. I am the only one left, and now they are trying to kill me too."
>
> The Lord said, "Go out and stand on the mountain in the presence of the Lord, for the Lord is about to pass by."
>
> Then a great and powerful wind tore the mountains apart and shattered the rocks before the Lord, but the Lord was not in the wind. After the wind there was an earthquake, but the Lord was not in the earthquake. After the earthquake came a fire, but the Lord was not in the fire. And after the fire came a gentle whisper. When Elijah heard it, he pulled his cloak over his face and went out and stood at the mouth of the cave.
>
> Then a voice said to him, "What are you doing here, Elijah?" (1 Kings 9:9-13)

The Prophet Elijah didn't find God in the mighty wind, the earthquake, or the fire, but in the small voice. In my early years as a Christian, I had a pretty good understanding of who God the Father and God the Son were and what they did. But I didn't understand the Person or role of the Holy Spirit. I thought He was some kind of cosmic Casper the friendly ghost. But then I read where Jesus told His disciples, "But the Counselor, the Holy Spirit, whom the Father will send in My name, will teach you all things and will remind you of everything I have said to you" (John 14:26).

A bit later, Jesus told them, "It is for your good that I am going away. Unless I go away, the Counselor will not come to you; but if I go, I will send Him to you. When He comes, He will convict the world of guilt. . . . [H]e will guide you into all truth. . . . He will bring glory to Me by taking from what is Mine and making it known to you" (John 16:7-8, 13-14).

The Apostle Paul wrote, "No eye has seen, no ear has heard, no mind has conceived what God has prepared for those who love Him." But the exciting thing is that God has revealed it to us by His Spirit. Paul went on to say, "The Spirit searches all things, even the deep things of God. . . . [N]o one knows the thoughts of God except the Spirit of God. We have not received the spirit of the world but the Spirit who is from God, that we may understand what God has freely given us" (1 Cor. 2:9-12).

After many years of being a Christian, reading God's Word, studying the Book of Acts, and counseling Christians, it has become clear to me that God the Holy Spirit plays a unique role during our difficult times. Jeffrey Jernigan gave us a wonderful illustration of how the Spirit helps us learn from failure:

Some years ago I was learning to fly. Like most young pilot candidates, I was confident, aggressive and overly sure of myself. I was going to master the skills required without outside interference or help.

Everything went fine until we got to the night part. Flying in the dark is scary! The instructor and I zoomed down the runway in waning twilight for my first night flight. By the time we had been in the air for an hour, it was pitch black outside. Our exercises had taken us into the country, and the ground was a formless, depthless black soup. I was lost, and no one had left his lights on for me!

Finally, after struggling with the instruments, I got the plane on course for the airport. We were going to land at a "real" airport at night, not the friendly training field I was used to. The instructor offered to help when I was clearly lost, and each time I refused.

After I had successfully slipped into the traffic pattern and established communications with the air traffic controller without a major foul-up, I felt pretty cocky. Now I was ready to land. The instructor asked if I wanted the REIL lights fired up. These are the strobe lights that mark the end of the runway by flashing in a sequence that points in the direction of the runway and illuminates where you touch down. Confident of my approach, I said "no."

As if reading the instructor's mind, the controller came over the radio asking if I would like the REIL lights turned on. Again I egotistically said "no!" I should have known that they were aware of something I had completely missed! Without another word the controller turned on the lights. Since we were so low, the cockpit filled with the reflected glare of these flashing strobe lights . . . not in front of me . . . but moving from left to right directly beneath my airplane. I was flying perpendicular to the runway, lined up on the parking lot of a local high school.

Sufficiently humbled, I cleared the pattern and set up for another approach. This time I responded to the controller's directions for changes in heading and altitude.

This pictures for me the Holy Spirit's role in our failures. So that I could land safely, both my will and the controller's will had to be active and participating; each of us had to be doing our assigned tasks. If either of us failed to do so, disaster would result. In Galatians 5:16-18 we read, "Walk by the Spirit. . . . [Be] led by the Spirit."[5]

Avoid the temptation to look too far down the road. Don't tell God what you think you need. Ask what *He* thinks you need. Ask what He wants to give you. Don't ask Him to move that mountain; look for how He wants to help you grow through your circumstances to accomplish His purpose in your life. Pray, "Lord, in this situation, what does it mean for me to trust and obey You? What do You want me to learn and do?" As you obey what you know to be true, you'll experience His presence and power. But never forget that His blessing is always preceded by obedience.

If you've taken these first three steps, you're probably surprised at how much better you're feeling. But don't stop here. The process of sanctification isn't about feeling better. It's about learning and maturing. It's about changing. Don't settle for a Band-Aid when God wants to give you so very much more.

Step 4: Align Your Perspective to His

In James 1, the brother of Jesus wrote, "When all kinds of trials and temptations crowd into your lives . . . don't resent them as intruders, but welcome them as friends! Realize that they come to test your faith and to produce in you the quality of endurance. But let the process go on until that endurance is fully developed, and you will find you have become [people] of mature character . . . with no weak spots" (James 1:2-4, PH).

In Romans, the Apostle Paul wrote, "And we rejoice in the hope of the glory of God. Not only so, but we also rejoice in our sufferings, because we know that suffering produces perseverance; perseverance, character; and character, hope. And hope does not disappoint us, because God has poured out His love into our hearts by the Holy Spirit, whom He has given us" (Rom. 5:2b-5).

We've already seen that God's perspective on our failure includes His desire to help us grow through it and bring good out of it. It's difficult to appreciate that when we're in the pits, of course, yet it's essential that we seek to look at the situation through His eyes. As Oswald Chambers wrote:

Are you severely troubled right now? Are you afraid and confused by the waves and the turbulence God sovereignly allows to enter your life? Have you left no stone of your faith unturned, yet still not found any well of peace, joy, or comfort? Does your life seem completely barren to you? Then look up and receive the quiet contentment of the Lord Jesus. Reflecting His peace is proof that you are right with God, because you are exhibiting the freedom to turn your mind to Him. . . . Allowing anything to hide the face of Jesus Christ from you (including failure) causes you to become even more troubled.

With regard to the problem that is pressing in on you right now, are you "looking unto Jesus" (Hebrews 12:2)? We become troubled because we have not been taking Him into account.[6]

Time and again, we see things only through our eyes rather than allowing Him to help us look through His. When God called Moses to serve Him, Moses gave God a list of all the reasons why he wasn't a good candidate. In chapters 3 and 4 of Exodus, he said:

3:11	I'm not much.
3:13	I won't have anything impressive to say.
4:1	I'm not real convincing.
4:10	I'm not a great speaker. I'm slow of speech and slow of tongue.
4:13	Anybody will do a better job than me, or "Lord, what is it about my being a loser that You don't understand?"

If you look at each one of those references, you'll find that God had a response for each of Moses' concerns. Basically God said, "That's great! You're just the kind of person I was looking for. I think I can use you."

When God called Jeremiah, his first response was, "I do not

know how to speak; I am only a child." But God said, "Don't worry about it. I'll go with you; I'll tell you what to say; I'll protect you" (Jer. 1:4-10, my paraphrase).

God knew they were weak and would make mistakes. God knows *we're* weak and will make mistakes. But as we align our perspective to His, we'll understand the process, reach out for His hand, and make it to the next step.

I was born in Montana but grew up on the beaches of Southern California. As a young boy, one of my greatest thrills was to head up to Montana to visit my relatives. Two of my uncles had ranches outside of Great Falls, and I could easily fill a day exploring the ranch, getting acquainted with the different chickens, pigs, horses, and cattle, climbing on haystacks, or playing "ditchum" with my cousins.

During one of my visits, my uncle asked if I wanted to see the birth of a calf. "Sure!" I said with enthusiasm. He explained that it was very important for someone to be on hand for a birth. Even during the dead of winter, he would check on the cows to be sure to be present during a birth. He said that sometimes the mother can struggle and lose the calf.

When the calf was born, it was wet and wobbly and struggled to get up on its toothpick-thin legs. It made several unsuccessful attempts before I asked, "Aren't you going to help it?"

My uncle looked at me with a smile and replied, "Gary, that would be the worst thing I could do. Those early struggles to stand and breathe on its own are vital to life." He told me that if we tried to help the little calf stand up, it could actually hurt the calf. That didn't make sense to me. But he went on to explain that when a calf is born, the effort involved in trying to get on its feet, the struggle to breathe, and the search for the mother's milk all provide it with the strength and stamina necessary for survival.

As I look back on that experience, it's obvious that, much like the little calf, we need the struggle and effort of failure to help us develop the skills and stamina to become mature men and women. When we have God's perspective, when we put our situation in the context of who He is and what He can do, things will begin to look different. We'll begin to see a way out. Failure is just another situation He can and will use in a constructive way for our growth.

Step 5: Acknowledge the Anatomy of Failure

At this point, it's important to pause for a moment and remind ourselves of the anatomy of failure. Why? Because when we're face-to-face with discouragement and defeat, it's easy for the reality of those painful emotions to block out everything else.

Although we've asked God to help us see things from His perspective, it doesn't mean that the pain is magically going to vanish. The fog of confusion may not instantly lift. We'll still have to walk through the process. That's how growth takes place. And rather than being confused by what's taking place, we'll know what's normal and what isn't.

In chapter 3, we talked at length about the three phases of dealing with failure: the crisis phase, the crossroads phase, and the catalyst phase. It's usually somewhere in the middle of the crisis phase that people begin to reach out for help. Remember, when we're in the crisis phase, we're riding an emotional roller coaster. This phase is characterized by denial, resistance, shock, fear, anger, guilt, shame, despair, confusion, and disorientation.

Even when we come to the crossroads phase and choose to respond to God's offer for help, we will still experience painful feelings. Most of us would rather bypass the crisis phase. Unfortunately, we can't. But we can dramatically shorten how long we stay there. We can spin our wheels and get deeper in the rut, or we can trust and obey and choose to grow.

At this point, we've taken the first five steps for growing through failure. We've already made tremendous progress, allowing God to help us turn the corner. In the next chapter, we'll continue our look at this process that will enable us to turn our setbacks into comebacks.

Small Beginnings

1. In your own words, why is waiting until you're in the middle of a crisis the worst time to learn how to deal with failure?

2. Think of a time when you had a definite sense of God's presence in your life. What difference did it make to you? How can you remember that experience the next time you fail?

3. If you want to have a good time, get out your personal calendar and set aside fifteen minutes sometime in the next twenty-four hours to simply praise the Lord. Thank Him for His love, mercy, goodness, faithfulness, and forgiveness. Praise Him for all the ways He has guarded, guided, protected, and provided for you. I promise you'll be surprised by how quickly those fifteen minutes go by.

4. James 4:2 says we don't have because we don't ask. In what area of your life do you need God's direction right now? Once a day for the next thirty days, give that request to Him in prayer. Also ask three friends to join you in prayer for that need.

6. Getting through Failure
Part 2

You'll recall that in our first session, Mary told me, "I was a failure as a wife. I'm a failure as a mom, I'm a failure as an employee, and I'm a failure as a Christian. It seems like the harder I try, the worse things get. I don't know what to do. I don't know where to start. And I don't really know if I even care."

She was overwhelmed with feelings of hopelessness and helplessness. By the end of step five, however, Mary was in a different place. "Mary, what's different? What in your life has changed?" I asked.

Without missing a beat, she replied, "I have more energy and more hope, and I know I'm not alone."

"So *everything* is better?" I asked.

She laughed and with a smile replied, "There are still times when I'm discouraged and feel a lot of guilt and pain. But it doesn't happen as much as it used to. And the feelings aren't as intense as they were when I started." Finally, in a voice filled with conviction and clarity, she said, "I know I still have more work to do. And I know some of it will be painful. But I know that with God's help, I can do it!"

That's not the comment of someone who has faced failure

and retreated to a Pollyanna-like dreamland of make-believe peace. That's not the conviction of someone who is blaming the world for all her problems. That's the comment of someone who has taken God's hand, stared failure in the face, and chosen to walk through it — someone who has the perspective and confidence that only God can give.

If you made it through steps one through five, the stage has been set. You're ready to move on. But there aren't any shortcuts. Without completing those five foundational steps, it's almost impossible to complete the growth process.

Step 6: Admit You Made a Mistake

When God finally gets your attention and makes you see you've made a mistake, there are two responses you must avoid at all costs. The first is to deny it. That's been my most common response. That's how my sons respond: "I didn't do it, Dad! Honest!"

We don't like for people to see the flaws in our character. We try to hide failure the way an adolescent tries to hide his blemishes. When I was in tenth grade, I had what in retrospect was a mild case of the zits. Of course, when they're on your face, and when you're in tenth grade in a new high school, they're a severe case with proportions similar to Mount Everest. I tried everything I could find to hide them or heal them, but nothing worked.

In the first chapter, we talked about how, when Adam and Eve sinned, their first response was to try to hide from God. They also tried to hide their nakedness from each other. But whenever we run from failure, we're really only trying to hide from ourselves. It doesn't matter how clever we are. It doesn't matter how many ways we have to medicate and anesthetize ourselves. The rationalization and deception can only last so long. At some point, the truth will come out.

The other response to avoid is the blame response. My kids know that if I don't buy the "I didn't do it, Dad" routine, the next-best option is to point to one of their brothers and say, "He did it!" That's exactly what Adam and Eve did. They tried to hurl the blame for their sin on someone else. It didn't work for them, however, it hasn't worked for me (or my boys), and it won't work for you.

Thus, a critical step in learning from failure is choosing to avoid the temptation to hide or hurl. Instead, we must look to God for the courage and conviction to admit it. Remember that most of us have been conditioned by parents, teachers, and friends to feel stupid or even afraid when we make a mistake. If our mistake came in the package of a failure, we can expect embarrassment and perhaps even some form of punishment.

I once heard a speaker say that "failure can be a weight or it can give you wings." Since an occupational hazard of being human is that we'll make mistakes, we're almost daily faced with a choice. We can let our failures drag us down and demoralize us, or we can choose to see them as an opportunity to learn and grow.

Gordon MacDonald describes a group of people he calls the secret carriers of the past. He says they have "an active memory of an event or events in the past for which they have consuming regret. They live in the constant fear that their secret will come back to haunt them with consequences that will shatter not only their worlds but the worlds of loved ones and trusted friends. . . . Secret carriers expend tremendous psychic and emotional energy to keep the past from interfering with the present. . . . Active secret carriers become experts in deception to survive." After a while, such a person's secrets "have become secrets even to him. He lives with these destructive performances and attitudes day after day until they simply blend with every other part of his life just as hair grew through the fabric of a hat."[1]

"Self-knowledge, the beginning of wisdom, is ruled out for most people by the increasingly effective self-deception they practice as they grow older," said John Gardner. "By middle age, most of us are accomplished fugitives from ourselves. Yet there's a surprising usefulness in learning not to lie to your-self."[2]

And we must be careful not to candy coat our mistakes. There's a story about a woman who had acquired great wealth and social prominence. She hired a well-known author to write a book about her genealogy. In the process of researching her family tree, this author discovered that one of her grandfathers was a murderer who had been electrocuted in Sing Sing Prison. When he said this would have to be included in the book, the woman pleaded with him to find a way of saying it that would disguise the truth.

When the book was published, the incident read as follows: "One of her grandfathers occupied the chair of applied electricity in one of America's best-known institutions. He was very much attached to his position and literally died in the harness."

In my introductory course in psychology, I was fascinated by the behavioral learning experiments with rats. In one experiment, a psychologist places a rat in a box with a grilled metal floor. The grill is hooked up to an electric current so that it can shock the rat's paws. Inside the box is a pedal that, when pressed, will cause the electric shock to stop. When placed in the box, the rats would squeal, run, jump, and paw at the grill. In time, however, they would press the pedal, and the shock would stop. After the tenth trial, the average rat would go directly to the pedal and press it.

Through a sequence of trial and error, the rats had learned how to make the correct response. How did this learning take place? During the first nine trials, they suffered various degrees of failure. And each failure had a painful consequence. They learned that jumping, running, squealing, and pawing at the grill didn't work. At some point, they decided to try something else.

When I read about this research, my first response was, "What a bunch of smart rats they had! It only took them ten tries to get it down." More times than I care to recall, it's taken me many more than ten "trials" to learn the lesson God was patiently trying to teach me.

If your failure was one that involved sin, there's an additional step you must take. First John 1:9 says, "If we confess our sins, He is faithful and just and will forgive us our sins and purify us from all unrighteousness." It's one thing to feel sad about sin. Anyone can do that. It's an entirely different thing to come before God in prayer and confess our sin.

Oswald Chambers wrote, "It is *not being reconciled to the fact of sin* that produces all the disasters in life. . . . If we refuse to take the fact of sin into our calculation, refuse to agree that a base impulse runs through men, that there is such a thing as vice and self-seeking, when our hour of darkness strikes, instead of being acquainted with sin and the grief of it, we will compromise straight away and say there is no use battling against it."[3]

In his second letter to the Christians in Corinth, Paul said he was rejoicing over the fact that they had moved from sorrow to repentance. "Godly sorrow brings repentance that leads to salvation and leaves no regret, but worldly sorrow brings death" (2 Cor. 7:10). The noun Paul used for *repentance* doesn't mean that they felt better about it; it means they now had a new mind.

Repentance is one of those old-fashioned words we don't hear often. It's not what we would call a politically correct term. Yet it contains a key to understanding how we can become godly men and women. Repentance doesn't come easily for any of us, especially in today's culture. Why? In part because repentance involves taking responsibility. As we've seen, people are no longer responsible; they're victims. They no longer sin; they just have problems.

But true Christianity goes beyond sorrow to confession and repentance. As Eugene Peterson wrote:

Repentance is not an emotion. . . . It is a decision. It is deciding that you have been wrong in supposing that you could manage your own life and be your own god; it is deciding that you were wrong in thinking that you had, or could get, the strength, education and training to make it on your own; it is deciding that you have been told a pack of lies about yourself and your neighbors and your world. And it is deciding that God in Jesus Christ is telling you the truth. Repentance is a realization that what God wants from you and what you want from God are not going to be achieved by doing the same old things, thinking the same old thoughts.[4]

In the same vein, Gordon MacDonald wrote:

Repentance is not a one-time act; it is actually a spiritual life-style. To live in a constant state of repentance is to acknowledge that the heart is always ready to drift into wrong directions and must constantly be jerked back to control. This is not a call to a morbid kind of introspection that is always on a sin-search, putting ourselves down, but it is an honest recognition that the inward part of us is inclined toward rebellion and disobedience against our Maker. And it will always be that way until the end of time.[5]

Recently, a well-known gospel singer apologized for an adulterous relationship with another famous Christian musician that, at least for the present, ended both of their careers in that field. In a press release, she candidly admitted her failure. "I am deeply grieved that so much of the public has been subjected to the private matters and failings of my life," she said. "I am extremely sorry for what I have done and the great number of people who have been hurt."

She acknowledged that "because of the mistakes I have made, I realize that continuing in this arena is not possible." She continued, "I take full responsibility for the choices I have made and for the consequences they bring." Finally she concluded, "My prayer is that what I have done would not bring discredit to what I have always sung about and believed in, but credibility to the reality that we are all weak and fail in our attempts to be righteous. Jesus died and paid the penalty we could not pay, and my hope rests there. I am living proof that there is unconditional love, grace and mercy for all of us."

Our willingness to embrace the truth about our failures controls our capacity for change and growth. It will determine the degree to which God will bless us.

Step 7: Accept Responsibility for It

It's one thing to admit you made a mistake; it's another thing to have the courage to accept responsibility for it, like that singer. Consider the following examples:

> Pauline Zile tried to cover up the murder of her daughter. But it was really John Aile's fault.
>
> Clover Boykin says she killed her son. But it was really her father's fault.
>
> The Menendez brothers killed their parents. But it was really the parents' fault.
>
> An FBI agent, fired for stealing money he then lost on bets, won his job back when a judge ruled him a victim of compulsive gambling.
>
> A man on trial for murder claims a sleep disorder made him shoot his wife to death.
>
> A Lebanese man who shot and killed two Hasidic Jews in New York says he did so because he was emotionally scarred by his childhood in Beirut.

America used to be known as the land of the free and the home of the brave. Today it is known as the land of the guilt-free, fault-free, and responsibility-free. We're reaping the harvest of situation ethics run amok. It doesn't seem to matter what happened, everybody is a victim. It was really someone else's fault. This victim mentality leads to whining rather than winning. It's true that Christ turned water into wine, but it's hard to turn a whiner into anything of value or good taste.

With candor and clarity, Haddon Robinson wrote:

> Adam and Eve's descendants—especially those in the United States—have refined victimization to a fine art and an article of faith. . . . If you want to get rich, invest in victimization. It is America's fastest growing industry. Millions make a fat paycheck by identifying victims, representing victims, interviewing victims, treating victims, insuring victims, counseling victims, preaching to victims, and, of course, being victims.
>
> The difficulty that Adam and Eve faced was that their Creator was not a talk-show host. If they were to indulge in the forbidden fruit today, Geraldo or Donahue would feature them as victims, the serpent would be their enabler, and some lawyer would be waiting in the wings to assure them they had a strong case to bring against God for damages.[6]

The sad thing is that the victimization mentality causes us to look for a scapegoat rather than a Savior. If I'm not responsible for what I do, if someone else is always to blame, I don't need a Savior. The other person does. Our culture has changed the words to the old spiritual that used to read, "Not my mother or my father, but it's me, O Lord, standing in the need of prayer." Now we sing, "It's my mother, it's my father, it's not me, O Lord, standing in the need of prayer." But truly successful people have learned how to recognize their mistakes, admit them, and accept responsibility.

Step 8: Analyze What Happened

What we do at this point helps us move beyond recovery to discovery, beyond survival to success. Step eight involves asking ourselves a series of questions. Usually the failure that knocks us off our feet isn't something that's never happened before. It may have occurred with less intensity or under slightly different circumstances. Perhaps the consequences weren't as great. But we've "been there, done that" before. Unfortunately, we didn't learn from those experiences. So our loving Heavenly Father is allowing us to take the course again until we get a passing grade.

The first set of questions involves looking back. To analyze your own failure, take out a clean sheet of paper, get a pencil, put your Bible within reach, and ask yourself these questions:

Has this ever happened before?

When was it?

How did I respond?

What did I do that didn't work?

What didn't I learn that I could have?

Sometimes you'll have a dramatic revelation. At other times, you may only notice seemingly small insights. Both are valuable. For example, maybe you noticed a series of small activities that made you more vulnerable to other choices that rendered you almost powerless to temptation.

Frequently the things that set us up for failure aren't in themselves sinful. Having one more cookie, keeping the TV remote in my hand as I channel surf, lingering over an HBO movie, and staying up to watch David Letterman aren't sin. But if I'm struggling with obesity, if I spend too much time in front of the TV, if my thought life is weakened by that movie I'm watching, or if staying up late keeps me from getting up in the morning to have that essential time with the Lord . . . then these seemingly harmless activities can set me up for, and make me more vulnerable to, sin.

When I find myself starting to rationalize with "It's not that bad," "But I couldn't help myself," "Well, it could have been a lot worse," or the perennial favorite, "Yeah, but look at what I'm *not* doing," I'm walking on thin ice.

As we saw at the start of chapter 5, Mary's "dark night of the soul" wasn't caused by any one event. It was the cumulative effect of several events that brought on her crisis. However, she felt especially convicted by her involvement with her non-Christian friend. She knew that fornication was sin, and she had confessed and repented.

"Now what do I do?" she asked.

I said her next step was to look back and analyze what happened. "The purpose of step eight," I told her, "is to mine this mistake for all the gold you can find."

As we studied what had happened, she realized she had both compromised and rationalized principles she knew to be true. For example, Proverbs 4:23 says, "Above all else, guard your heart, for it is the wellspring of life." *The Living Bible* makes it even clearer: "Above all else, guard your affections. For they influence everything else in your life."

"I knew Proverbs 4:23," Mary said. "In fact, I taught it to my kids. But for a brief moment in time, I forgot it."

"Forgot it?" I asked.

She smiled and said, "Well, I didn't really forget it. I guess I chose to ignore it." And that's all it took.

After mining previous failures, turn your attention to your present state. Ask yourself:

What did I do wrong?

What did I do that set me up for failure?

What excuses did I allow myself to make?

What did I do that weakened my resistance?

What did my conscience try to tell me that I ignored?

What did I do that made me more vulnerable to sin?

Chapter 2 discussed the most common causes for failure. If you get stuck here, you may want to turn back to that chapter.

Step 9: Assess What You Could Do Differently Next Time

If you were to walk into a room and see me flicking the light switch up and down a couple of times, you probably wouldn't think anything about it. However, if you walked into the same room again fifteen minutes later and I was still standing there flicking the switch, you would probably have some concerns about my mental condition. Why? Well, if the light doesn't come on after the first or second try, what is there to make me believe it will come on after the 247th? Nothing. It would be crazy for me to stand there and continue flicking that switch. It's just as crazy for you or me to continue making choices that lead to sin and failure. My favorite definition of crazy is this: "Crazy is to find out what doesn't work and keep on doing it."

Some people go through life hostage to the futile hope that if they do something the same way they have before, somehow it will turn out differently the next time. Sometimes it may, but usually it won't. Every time we experience failure, we've come face-to-face with an opportunity to learn something. In step eight, you analyzed what happened, what worked, and what didn't. In step nine you ask yourself, "What's the message in the failure? What can I learn from this? I know what doesn't work. What can I do differently?"

Learning involves trying something different. Whenever we try something different, we may make mistakes. But without mistakes there's no learning. Yet some people make mistakes and never learn, so we need to do more than make mistakes. We need to develop a way of looking at ourselves and our mistakes and have a plan for mining those mistakes for life lessons.

Thomas Edison said, "Results! Why, man, I have gotten a lot of results. I know several thousand things that won't work."

Successful people frequently risk failure. I heard one motivational speaker say, "If you want to double your success ratio, you have to double your failure rate." Mistakes are inevitable anyway. And every time you make a mistake and choose to learn from it, it builds strength and character and leads to growth.

When I was in elementary school, I loved to play the game Twenty Questions. I've heard that some teachers still use it to help children learn to think logically. Let me refresh your memory about how the game is played.

The challenge might be to guess a number between 1 and 1,000. The object is to guess the correct number in 20 yes-or-no questions or less. In playing this game, I never remember anyone getting the correct answer after the first question. The key to the game is to learn from each wrong guess and narrow the possibilities, finally arriving at the correct answer by the time you get to the twentieth question.

Children who've never been taught the value of failure can be traumatized by this simple game. For example, if they ask, "Is the number between 500 and 1,000?" and the reply is yes, they smile and cheer. But if the answer is no, they get a discouraged look and groan, even though they get exactly the same amount of information in either case. One teacher reports that the more anxious students will repeatedly ask questions that have already been answered, just for the satisfaction of hearing a yes.[7]

Many children (and adults) hang on to the idea that the only good answer is a yes. That's the unfortunate result of their miseducation in which "right answers" are the only ones that pay off. They never learned how to learn from a mistake, or even that learning from mistakes is possible.

Now let's apply this learning principle from the Twenty Questions game to real life. What do you do when you don't know what to do? The first move is to go back to step eight and make sure you've learned all you can from previous failures. If you want to know what might work, rule out what you know hasn't worked.

Then you might want to seek the counsel of some wise friends. Have they ever been in a similar situation? What did they do? What worked, and what didn't? What did they learn? Proverbs tells us there is wisdom in many counselors (see Prov. 15:22).

If, after going over these steps, you still don't know what to do, don't do anything. Apparently God wants you to wait a bit longer. When you aren't sure about something, do something you *are* sure about. Turn to the Lord in prayer. Read the Bible. Remember the basics. Be filled with the Holy Spirit. Let your life be characterized by the fruit of the Spirit.

You can let go of the failure by deciding what you need to do now and what you can do differently next time. You don't need to wait until the situation arises. You can pull a friend aside and role play the new response with him or her. If you practice a response when you're not under pressure, you'll be much more likely to make the healthy response when you *are* under pressure.

Step 10: Accept God's Forgiveness

I enjoy snow skiing. I'm not pretty to watch, but I have a lot of fun getting down to the bottom of the mountain. One of the many benefits of living at the foot of the Rocky Mountains is that you're close to great snow and exceptional slopes.

Last year I went skiing with my friend Jim Tallant. Jim had been a ski instructor and on the ski patrol, so I was looking forward to getting a few hints on how to improve my form. After watching me go down a couple of runs, Jim said, "Gary, you have great potential. Your main problem is your poor perspective." He went on to tell me that I looked down at my skis too much.

"If I don't watch them," I asked, "how will I know if they're going where they're supposed to?"

Jim replied, "Has looking at your skis kept you from falling?" We both knew the answer to that question. He continued, "When you go down this time, try to look out at the view in front of you. If you keep your eyes on the mountains, you'll be more likely to keep your balance." Do you know something? He was right. What I had been doing wasn't working, but I had kept on doing it. Jim challenged me to do something different. A change in my perspective changed my performance.

What works in snow skiing also works in dealing with failure. When we fall, our natural tendency is to focus on our failure, dwell on our disappointments, and get stuck in our setback. As we learn how to adjust our actions to how God would have us respond, things become much simpler.

If you've sinned, confess it, repent of it, and learn all you can from it so that it doesn't happen again. Choose to receive and accept God's forgiveness. At times it's easy to forgive the failures of others. But when it comes to our own, we can be merciless. I spent years beating myself up over stupid, sinful, and selfish things I'd done. I knew that God forgave me, but I couldn't forgive myself.

If you've wronged others, apologize to them and ask for their forgiveness. If you need to make restitution, get to it eagerly and quickly.

If you were wronged by others, follow the guidelines of Matthew 18 and confront them. If they're healthy enough to admit their mistake and ask for your forgiveness, give it to them. Even if they don't ask for your forgiveness, it's in your best interest and that of God's kingdom if you choose to forgive them anyway. Don't be a martyr. Don't milk it.

Step 11: Activate Your Plan

In Psalm 5, David begged the Lord to tell him what to do: "Give ear to my words, O Lord. . . . Listen to my cry for help" (vv. 1-2). We've already taken that step, but in my own life, that's usually the easiest one. The hardest step is the one we're on right now—doing what God tells me to do. I've struggled much more with knowing the right thing to do and not doing it than I have with not knowing what to do.

We've asked ourselves the question, "What can I do differently?" We've prayed about it. We've thought about it. We may have talked with friends about it. We've rehearsed it. Now, in the words of that Nike commercial, we need to "Just Do It!" and be on the lookout for the first opportunity to apply what we've learned.

Satan loves to play with our minds. He torments us with trivialities. He encourages an oversensitive conscience that allows us no peace. He delights in leading us down the primrose path of endless self-examinations. Let's not wait for the "perfect" time to begin. *Now* is always the best time to put into practice what God has taught us.

When we come to the inevitable valley experiences of life, when we feel deprived of faith and assurance, when we lack the confidence or energy to take the last step, there's only one thing we can do. We must by faith take the next step. We must walk through that valley and trust that He who promised to never leave us or forsake us is being faithful to His promise. Hebrews 12:1-3 is a wonderful passage in this regard:

> Therefore, since we are surrounded by such a great cloud of witnesses, let us throw off everything that hinders and the sin that so easily entangles, and let us run with perseverance the race marked out for us. Let us fix our eyes on Jesus, the author and perfecter of our faith, who for the joy set before Him endured the cross, scorning its shame, and sat down at the right hand of the throne of God. Consider Him who endured such opposition from sinful men, so that you will not grow weary and lose heart.

From that passage we can derive the following checklist:

- Remind yourself of the example of faithful men and women who have gone before you.
- Throw off everything that might hinder you or slow you down.
- Run with perspiration and perseverance.
- Don't be surprised if you get a little weary.
- Keep your eyes fixed on Jesus.

For many people, putting their plan into action becomes the last step. Big mistake! There's one more important step we must take to complete the growth process.

Step 12: Announce What God Has Taught You

The important last step in the process of growing through failure is to share with those around you the lessons you've learned. Dr. Harold Englund had the right idea in saying, "When I lay an egg, I autograph it and hold it up for all to see." He realized that one of the best ways to keep ourselves accountable to what God has taught us and to share the encouragement of His faithfulness is to announce our victory.

But when you make your announcement, don't announce what *you* did. Proclaim what *God* did. There's a big difference. I've heard some testimonies where 90 percent of the focus was on the delicious details of their sinful past, and only the last 10 percent pointed to Christ. They seemed to get greater joy talking about "the wages of sin" than they did about "the gift of God."

In the Old Testament, when God did a significant work for His people, they often built a physical marker to remind them of it. For example, when the Children of Israel crossed the Jordan River into the Promised Land, God told Joshua, "Choose twelve men from among the people, one from each tribe, and tell them to take up twelve stones from the middle of the Jordan from right where the priests stood and to carry them over with you and put them down at the place where you stay tonight" (Josh. 4:2-3).

The pile was a visual reminder of what God had done. Joshua explained, "In the future, when your children ask you, 'What do these stones mean?' tell them that the flow of the Jordan was cut off before the ark of the covenant of the Lord. When it crossed the Jordan, the waters of the Jordan were cut off. These stones are to be a memorial to the people of Israel forever" (Josh. 4:6-7).

Such markers may have been built to commemorate a lesson learned, a direction given, a goal achieved, or God's special guidance received during a difficult time of transition or decision-making. You may be surprised to discover that markers can be as helpful to us today as they were for the Children of Israel 3,000 years ago. A marker can be a valuable way to announce the significant things God has taught us from our failures. For each of my markers, God gave me a special verse. You may or may not have a verse associated with your significant failures, but there's undoubtedly some spiritual principle that God wanted to teach you or remind you of. So you may also want to erect some physical memorials like those biblical people.

I have several such markers. The one people ask me about the most is rather unusual. It comes from a time when things were going great for me. My counseling ministry was growing. I was writing a book. I was doing radio interviews. I had more speaking opportunities than I could accept. And I was exhausted. I was doing God's good, but not God's best.

My motives were great, but I wasn't taking time to listen to the still, small voice of the Spirit. I heard it, but I wasn't paying attention. The pressure built and built. Things began to slip. The quality of my work decreased. The more out of control I felt, the more I tried to be in control. My friends didn't enjoy being around me. My wife and kids didn't, either. Even *I* didn't enjoy being around me!

After a long and difficult week, I began to realize how exhausted I really was. When I opened the Bible, God gave me two passages. Psalm 46:10 says, "Be still, and know that I am God." The words *be still* mean to cease your striving. Philippians 4:6-7 reads, "Do not be anxious about anything, but in everything, by prayer and petition, with thanksgiving, present your requests to God. And the peace of God, which transcends all understanding, will guard your hearts and your minds in Christ Jesus."

Reading those, I realized that, once again, my type-A, compulsive, and perfectionistic tendencies had taken over and placed me at risk of a physical breakdown. But more than that, they had put me in a place of significantly increased vulnerability to temptation and sin.

I asked God for a physical reminder of this important lesson. I waited in silence for a few minutes, and nothing came to me. After a few more minutes, I went upstairs to my son Matthew's bedroom to have a brief chat and give him the ritual back rub, prayer, and "mooch" that I give to each of my boys every night.

When I walked into his room, I heard his little hamster going wild on the treadmill. As I turned to look, something inside me said, "Gary, that's it! That's your marker." I remember smiling and thinking, *No, that's silly.* And of course, that's just the

point. So I went out and bought myself a little hamster treadmill, and I now have it sitting in my office.

Whenever I'm asked about that little treadmill, I can't help
but smile. God has used it to give me an opportunity to "announce" what He taught me to literally thousands of people.
Not only have I had the opportunity to explain the lessons of
Psalm 46:10 and Philippians 4:6-7, but each time I'm also given
a valuable refresher course in God's provision and faithfulness
and a reminder that my Lord is the Lord of my failures as well
as of my successes.

Satan wants us to focus on our failures. He takes every opportunity to stick our faces in the past. In fact, he would love
for us to remain firmly planted there. But God wants us to
remember what He taught us about Himself (and who we are
because we're in Him) through that failure. Satan wants us to
focus on what we lost. God wants us to focus on what we
learned. Satan wants us to feel the wound. God wants us to feel
the wonder of His faithfulness.

If you look at some of your significant failures over the past
several years, has there been a pattern? There was for me. It was
a pattern of overcommitment and poor use of time. God was
trying to teach me to put first things first, to learn how to say
no, to anchor my identity securely in Him, and to remember
that my acceptance was based on His completed work for me
on the cross, not on my performance, production, or ability to
please others.

Whatever the lessons God teaches you, make a point of an-
nouncing them to others, both verbally and through your own
memorial markers. Combined with the first eleven steps in this
chapter and the one preceding, they will help you not just to
survive failure, but to grow through it and make something
good out of it as well.

Small Beginnings

1. Take a look at some of your more recent failures, and ask
   yourself these simple questions:

Do you see similarities or patterns?

What significance do those patterns have for you?

Are they a simple sign of fallenness?

Are they God whispering a developing direction?

Are they a behavior you want to change?

Where will you be five years from now if you continue making the same mistakes?

2. In your own words, write a one-sentence summary of each of the twelve steps given in this chapter and the one before.

3. It was stated in this chapter that failure can be a weight or give you wings. Describe times when you've felt each and what you learned from those experiences.

7. Lessons Learned from Failure

America loves winners. Winners are important; losers aren't. Winners have friends; losers don't. Winners are happy; losers aren't. Winners have value; losers don't. That's why so much more is written about success than failure.

When I was a kid, I hated to lose. When I got married, I had a hard time when my wife would beat me in racquetball. When I became a father, I'm embarrassed to admit I even had a hard time losing games with my kids. Losing felt too much like failure, and I didn't like that feeling. But the older I get, the more I agree with Michael J. O'Neill, who wrote, "In its purest form, losing is one of mankind's highest callings. It is the primal element of progress. Failures preceded the great discoveries. Lost battles are as important as military victories. Centuries of error pave the way to advances in civilization. Defeat is the raw material from which champions are made."[1]

Let's take a look at someone many once considered a loser. You might have seen James Earl Jones in *Field of Dreams*. You probably remember hearing his voice as the diabolical Darth Vader in the three Star Wars films. I know your kids would remember his voice as Mufasa, the loving father lion, in *The Lion King*. He has won three Emmy Awards, two Tonys, a

Golden Globe, and a Grammy. What you probably don't know is that by the time he was fourteen, Jones was a gawky and shy teenager whose stutter was so pronounced that he never spoke in class. Not surprisingly, this insecure boy was a loner.

As a young boy, he was uprooted from his home in Mississippi to a farm near the tiny town of Dublin in northern Michigan. In many ways, it was an upward move for his family, but it was difficult nonetheless. "The whole journey meant a better education," Jones said. "A better world. A freer world. A less hateful world. But *I* was leaving a land that I loved."

Apparently the trauma of the move triggered his stutter. At times the effects of his stutter combined with his shyness to render him virtually mute. But he found friendship and understanding at his little one-room school in Dublin. At first he was able to communicate with his teacher and fellow students through notes. Then one day his English teacher, Donald E. Crouch, asked him to read a poem he had written. Can you imagine the fear that young James felt as he walked to the front of the room and began to speak? "To the astonishment of everyone, the words flowed smoothly. The stutter disappeared. He had stumbled upon what speech therapists would one day discover; that the scripted page could be a stutterer's salvation."

It was a major breakthrough for Jones. After his enormous victory that day, he decided to make speaking his challenge. With hours of hard work and practice, he became the high school's public-speaking champion. His speaking skills, combined with his good grades, earned him a scholarship to the University of Michigan.

When he got to the university, he felt "big, shy and ugly," so he joined a university drama group to gain self-confidence. After graduation and some time in the army, he moved in 1955 to New York to learn the craft of acting. He struggled for several years while he took acting lessons and played small roles in off-Broadway productions, supporting himself by working as a janitor with his father, cleaning out Broadway theaters and office buildings.

Over time, and with a lot of patience and perseverance, James Earl Jones became the honored and accomplished actor we know today. If you were to talk with him, he would tell you that the strength he gained through his early discouragements and "failures" played a major part in who he is and what he has become.[2]

Erwin Lutzer wrote that "failure is the back door to success." But if you're at all like me, you would much rather stroll through the front door. Sometimes it's just that easy. But at other times the front door appears to have been locked. Or worse yet, a guard has been posted in front of it and isn't about to let anyone in. If you have any hope of being successful, you'll have to take the long way around.

At some point in your life, you'll make a mistake and come face-to-face with some form of failure. And then, as I've said before, you're faced with a choice. What you decide at this point will either keep you *behind* the failure or allow you to grow *beyond* it. I should know. I spent many years playing it safe and living behind my failures. I didn't want to deal with the pain, face the embarrassment, or slow down my progress.

What happens when we refuse to learn from our failures? We end up repeating the same mistakes over again. We make more mistakes. Our "blind spots" grow larger. We end up making even bigger mistakes.

The other response is to choose to grow beyond the failure — to pan for the gold in our painful experiences, to "mine" them for everything we can. Sometimes it seems the most important lessons in life are the ones we already knew but somehow had allowed ourselves to forget.

In the midst of my losses, I gained a greater respect for the power of sin, a deeper appreciation of grace, an increased sensitivity to the weaknesses of myself and others, a new appreciation for the value of pain, and an increased effectiveness in my ministry. I learned that tragedy can lead to a healing vulnerability and openness, that in the midst of loss, God can create in us a new willingness to open up and share. After all, at this point we've got nothing to lose.

There's no intrinsic value in failure. It's foolish to try to fail. However, when we do fail, God wants to teach us. And that's what this chapter is about. As I searched the Scriptures, surveyed the literature, interviewed hundreds of men and women, and examined my own experience, I found ten core lessons that failure is very good at teaching us. Let me describe them to you.

1. There Are No Little Things

"Whoever can be trusted with very little can also be trusted with much, and whoever is dishonest with very little will also be dishonest with much" (Luke 16:10).

One of the major lessons we can learn from failure is that there are no little things. The majority of the failures in my life haven't been catastrophic but small and seemingly insignificant. Most often they didn't involve sin, only laziness, poor judgment, or compromise.

But those "little things" set me up for and made me more vulnerable to other decisions that got me a bit further from the "straight and narrow." The problem wasn't in my initial decisions. The problem was the direction they took me in and the perspective they robbed me of. A series of small and subtle changes can eventually lead to behaviors that will turn into failure.

Satan knows it will be hard to get us to turn dramatically. But he can get us to veer off the road. And then he can talk us into taking a "harmless" detour, into believing "it's not that bad." And he knows that if he can get us to take our eyes off our Lord—if he can seduce us into believing we can make it on our own—he has won a major victory. That's why it's so important to cultivate the habit of being faithful in little. If we do that, we won't have to worry about the "much."

2. Seek Jesus First

"But seek first His kingdom and His righteousness, and all these things will be given to you as well" (Matt. 6:33).

That's a well-known verse; you might have even memorized it. It's a simple principle that's even clearer in this popular paraphrase: "Steep your life in God-reality, God-initiative, God-provisions. Don't worry about missing out. You'll find all your everyday human concerns will be met."[3]

Sometimes we forget there is only one river of life, only one spring of living water, only one Person who can give long-lasting satisfaction, and that's Jesus. Only He can satisfy the hunger of our hearts and the thirst of our souls.

True success involves seeking God, loving God, considering God in everything, serving God in everything, and making every aspect of our lives holy by doing everything in His name and for His glory. The Bible tells us that true success starts with a love for God that's expressed in simple, ordinary, and small actions. As William Law wrote:

Our blessed Savior and his Apostles were very intent on giving us teachings that relate to daily life. They teach us:

to renounce the world and be different in our attitudes and ways of life;

to renounce all its goods, to fear none of its evils, to reject its joys, and have no value for its happiness;

to be as newborn babes who are born into a new state of things;

to live as pilgrims in spiritual watching, in holy fear, and heavenly aspiring after another life;

to take up our cross daily, to deny ourselves, to profess the blessedness of mourning, to seek the blessedness of poverty of spirit;

to forsake the pride and vanity of riches, to take no thought for the morrow, to live in the profoundest state of humility, to rejoice in worldly sufferings;

to reject the lust of the flesh, the lust of the eyes, and the pride of life;

to bear injuries, to forgive and bless our enemies, and to love all people as God loves them;

to give up our whole hearts and affections to God, and to strive to enter through the straight gate into a life of eternal glory.[4]

If you've been a Christian for more than a day, you've discovered it's a deadly error to try to live the Christian life by sheer willpower. Once you get a taste of the deep changes God wants to bring about, you'll see that His plan is so great that only He can supply what you need to accomplish it. Becoming a mature Christian requires constant fellowship with and dependence on Him for every need.

That's one reason those who have experienced the depths of failure are often the first to understand God's guaranteed formula for success. Those who appear to be always up, always happy, always successful are often the last to appreciate how God really works and what only He can do.

3. Prayer Changes Things

"Pray continually" (1 Thes. 5:17).

When Carrie and I were engaged, I couldn't spend enough time with her. We talked almost every day. When I wasn't with her, I was thinking about her. I looked forward with eager anticipation to each date. My motivation wasn't to check off my list "Date with Carrie." My motive was to be with her, talk to her, listen to her, and get to know her better. I spent time with her because I loved her.

In "The Rime of the Ancient Mariner," Samuel Taylor Coleridge wrote, "He prayeth well, who loveth well." I've discovered that real prayer, the deepest and most meaningful prayer, isn't motivated by shoulds and oughts, shame and guilt, or a desire to "pay our spiritual dues" so we can get on God's good side. It comes out of a heart of love for Him. I'm talking about an intimate, enduring, continuing, growing love relationship with Jesus Christ.

God longs for us to make it the top priority of our lives to learn to love Him with all our hearts — not perform for Him or accomplish great things for Him, but simply to love Him. One of the best ways to accomplish that is to have a daily time of communion with Him. Some people call this a quiet time.

For many years, I tried to have a consistent quiet time because I knew that's what spiritual people did, and I wanted desperately to be a spiritual person. In many ways, it was another thing on my "to do" list — another performance. Today it still takes an effort to be faithful in my morning time with God. But it's no longer the struggle it used to be. Why?

In part it's because I no longer get up just to have a quiet time. Instead, I get up to meet with God. There's a big difference between the two. God and I have an appointment every morning, and I know He's waiting for me. I don't keep my quiet time so that somehow God will love me more and then maybe I can have a relationship with Him. I keep my quiet time because I already have a relationship with Him, and I want it to grow. I keep my quiet time because it makes a dramatic difference in my day.

A critical part of my quiet time is prayer. Regular, consistent prayer moves us along the pathway to maturity. I believe that when we pray, we're ushered into the Holy of Holies. We're personally escorted to the foot of the throne of God. We're given an audience with the Creator of the universe. He's waiting. He's listening. He's eager to answer.

God wants to see us grow. He longs for us to experience a greater depth and intimacy of His love, and He delights in blessing us. The key that unlocks the door to His storehouse of blessing is prayer. As Richard Foster observed:

Today the heart of God is an open wound of love. He aches over our distance and preoccupation. He mourns that we do not draw near to him. He grieves that we have forgotten him. He weeps over our obsession with muchness and manyness. He longs for our presence.

And he is inviting you — and me — to come home, to

come home to where we belong, to come home to that for which we were created. His arms are stretched out wide to receive us. His heart is enlarged to take us in.

For too long we have been in a far country: a country of noise and hurry and crowds, a country of climb and push and shove, a country of frustration and fear and intimidation. And he welcomes us home: home to serenity and peace and joy, home to friendship and fellowship and openness, home to intimacy and acceptance and affirmation.

We do not need to be shy. He invites us into the living room of his heart, where we can put on old slippers and share freely. He invites us into the kitchen of his friendship, where chatter and batter mix in good fun. He invites us into the dining room of his strength, where we can feast to our heart's delight. He invites us into the study of his wisdom, where we can learn and grow and stretch . . . and ask all the questions we want. He invites us into the workshop of his creativity, where we can be co-laborers with him, working together to determine the outcomes of events. He invites us into the bedroom of his rest, where new peace is found and where we can be naked and vulnerable and free. It is also the place of deepest intimacy, where we know and are known to the fullest.[5]

4. Trust and Obey

"Trust in the Lord with all your heart and lean not on your own understanding; in all your ways acknowledge Him, and He will make your paths straight" (Prov. 3:5-6).

Many failures are caused by the fact that we don't trust God. The degree of trust we have in Him will determine what we do. And how we choose to respond to failure is an indicator of what we believe about Him and how much we trust Him.

God wants us to depend on Him—not our financial resources, quick wit, cleverness, charisma, educational degrees, years of experience, or litany of success, but *Him.*

It doesn't matter what we've done or where we find ourselves. We always have a choice. It's a part of our spiritual birthright. It reminds us that we were made in the image of God with attributes of intelligence, emotion, and will. We can choose to allow the events of life to carry us along as they will, bouncing us from rock to rock, pulling us downstream, or we can give up trying to do it on our own and surrender to Him.

But I've got to be honest with you. *Surrender* isn't one of my favorite terms. Trust me, however—when we're in the hands of a loving God, it can be one of life's sweetest experiences. You see, surrender doesn't mean we lost. It doesn't mean we're failures. It does mean handing over our need to play it safe and be in control to God. It means taking Him at His word and obeying Him. And it can lead to a new beginning.

Through the encounter with failure, our compulsion for being in control can be exposed and released. Unfortunately for some of us slow learners, the failure may need to be truly devastating before the courage to say "I surrender all" can manifest itself and prevail. But believe me, staying stuck, playing it safe, and going around in circles are vastly overrated.

There's no joy greater than that which comes from learning how to lean on the everlasting arms of a loving, faithful, and gracious Lord.

Lord,
I crawled
across the barrenness
to you
with my empty cup
uncertain
in asking
any small drop
of refreshment.
If only
I had known you
better

I'd have come
running
with a bucket.[6]

5. Cultivate Quality Criticism

"When a wise man is instructed, he gets knowledge" (Prov. 21:11).

Several years ago, someone told me that I came across as controlling and insensitive. My first response wasn't positive. But with a lot of help from God, I was able to listen, ask some clarifying questions, and get some examples. When I shared the observation with several friends, including my wife, they told me that part of it was true. Bummer!

In fact, my wife told me that while I had made some great improvements in this area, there were times when I still came across in a negative way. As we talked about it, I discovered I was more likely to appear controlling when I was tired or under a lot of pressure. That little piece of information was helpful. Now when I'm tired or pressured, I'm aware of this tendency, and I'm able to respond to people in ways that are more effective.

What's your first reaction to the word *criticism?* Is it positive or negative? My first response is negative. I don't like to be criticized. It exposes my flaws and makes me look bad. It means there's something I need to work on.

What about you? Come on, be honest! Do you listen carefully? Do you ask questions of your critic to make sure you clearly understand the concern? Do you invite the person to state any additional concerns? Do you express your appreciation to your critic for taking the time to help you become a better person?

You're probably a lot like me. Whenever we're criticized, we tend to get defensive, tune out what we don't want to hear, and focus on the other person's flaws. But in reality, our critics are the caution lights God puts along the road to maturity to help us avoid potholes and dead ends. Their motives may not be the best. The bulk of what they say may not be true. But even if only 1 percent of their criticisms is valid, I'm learning to seek out and listen to that 1 percent.

One of the greatest dangers of becoming successful is the tendency to discount or flat-out ignore negative information about ourselves. When that happens, real friendship — the iron sharpening iron kind of friendship — becomes impossible. The kind of honest information that's needed for our continued growth becomes scarce. The light that helps us stay on the straight and narrow becomes dim, and we begin to operate in increasing darkness. The successful leader gets only carefully filtered positive feedback and as a result becomes at increasing risk for unnecessary failure.

Gordon MacDonald told about one of his mentors who taught him that if he would always look for the kernel of truth in every criticism, he would be a better man for it. MacDonald wrote:

> Usually, in the past, I wasn't looking; I tended to be too busy ducking in self-defense. But as the time came when I could actually cultivate appreciation for criticism, my spiritual passion was enhanced.
>
> Now I am impressed by the fact that virtually everything of value I have learned has come from the mouths of my critics: both those who care for me and those who feel animosity toward me. When we look for the kernel of truth, we find growth, effectiveness, and room for spiritual passion.[7]

Healthy people have learned to value honest information. Make the time to cultivate close friends and quality critics whom you can trust to speak the truth in love.

6. When You Fail, God Can Forgive

"If we confess our sins, He is faithful and just and will forgive us our sins and purify us from all unrighteousness" (1 John 1:9).

One of the things I like the most about an electronic calculator is that if I enter the wrong information or get confused about where I'm at, all I have to do is push the "clear" button. Immediately all the information is cleared from the calculator. Then I'm able to begin again. I don't have to go back and try to sort out the previous mistake. In fact, there's no record of the previous mistake. It's lost forever.

That's what happens to our sins when God forgives us. Some of the pain and sorrow may remain, as well as some of the consequences. But the guilt—the legal condemnation for the offense—is gone! Our Lord is in the cleansing business, not the whitewashing business.

The consequences for not taking God at His word can be high. They include loss of confidence and joy, lack of victory and peace, and feelings of defeat, discouragement, and depression. Dr. Karl Menninger, the famous psychiatrist, said that if he could convince the patients in his psychiatric hospitals that their sins were forgiven, 75 percent of them could walk out the next day.

Thank God that what Satan designed to distract, discourage, and defeat us has now been turned into an opportunity for praise and thanksgiving. It has become a reminder of God's love, goodness, and faithfulness. In the past, the evil one has used our painful memories to rob us of our joy. But because God's Word is true, those same memories can remind us of the victory we have in Christ and actually increase our joy.

As a Christian, you don't have to go through life punishing yourself for sins you've confessed. You can stand on the reality of God's forgiveness. Psalm 103:12 says, "As far as the east is from the west, so far has He removed our transgressions from us." In the first two verses of Romans 8, we read, "There is therefore now no condemnation for those who are in Christ Jesus. For the law of the Spirit of life in Christ Jesus has set you free from the law of sin and of death" (NASB).

The story is told of a time many years ago when a father and his daughter were walking through the grass on the Canadian prairie. In the distance, they saw a prairie fire that would soon engulf them. The father knew there was only one way of escape: They had to quickly build a fire right where they were and burn a large patch of grass. Then, when the huge prairie fire drew near, they could stand on the section that had already been burned. When the flames did approach them, the girl was terrified, but her father assured her, "The flames can't get to us. We're standing where the fire has already been."

So it is with the forgiven. We're standing where the flames have already been, and we're safe. Jesus paid the price. We're forgiven.

7. It's Okay to Be Weak

"If I must boast, I will boast of the things that show my weakness" (2 Cor. 11:30).

That's a direct quote from the Apostle Paul. But can you imagine someone saying that today? What kinds of things do people usually boast about? That's right, their accomplishments and victories. What kinds of things do we deny and attempt to cover up? Our flaws and failures. But Paul said just the opposite. Not only is it okay to have weaknesses, but he even boasted about his.

Either Paul wasn't a very sharp guy or he knew something we don't. He had learned the values of struggle and failure from God's perspective, including the way they force us to look down into the depth of our humanity and discover the pockets of selfishness and pride that we weren't even aware of.

Christ told Paul, "My grace is sufficient for you, for My power is made perfect in weakness." Because of that Paul could say, "Therefore I will boast all the more gladly about my weaknesses, so that Christ's power may rest on me. That is why, for Christ's sake, I delight in weaknesses, in insults, in hardships, in persecutions, in difficulties. For when I am weak, then I am strong" (2 Cor. 12:9-10).

Paul was so confident in God's faithfulness and love, in His promises, and in what Christ had accomplished for him at the cross, that he was willing to risk failure. His confidence in Christ freed him to glory in his humanity that was being conformed to Christ. Paul "had no fear of failure because he had no fear of his potential to fail. He could accept his inevitable weaknesses because he understood that God's grace had already covered them all. In fact, Paul's weaknesses were the very channels through which the power of Christ could be manifested in his life."[8] And *our* weaknesses are the very channels through which the power of the risen Christ can be manifested through *our* lives!

8. Don't Give Up

"Let us not become weary in doing good, for at the proper time we will reap a harvest if we do not give up" (Gal. 6:9).

Dan Jansen isn't the only person to have fallen on the ice. Ice is slippery. One of the main reasons my boys like to go ice skating is to watch their dad fall. However, when you're a world-class speed skater, you aren't supposed to fall, especially at the Olympics. But Dan Jansen fell—twice in the 1988 Olympics and again in the 1992 Olympics.

When the 1994 Olympics rolled around, everyone thought that this time Jansen would surely win the men's 500-meter race. On Monday, February 14, 300 meters into the race, Jansen reached out to steady himself in a curve, and the friction of his hand scraping along the ice probably caused the thirty-five hundredths of a second's difference between the gold medal and Jansen's eighth-place finish. Thirty-five hundredths of a second!

When he stepped onto the Olympic ice again a few days later for the 1,000-meter race, Dan Jansen was 0-for-6 in all Olympic races. He was feeling out of sorts. He knew his timing was off. He struggled for traction. Seven competitors had already posted better times than Jansen's career best in the event. But this was going to be his last Olympic race, his last opportunity for a medal. His last chance to "prove" himself.

This wasn't his favorite event, either. His prospects didn't look good. But to the joy of millions of viewers in the United States, Dan Jansen won the 1,000 meters in world-record time, ending a decade-long saga of Olympic expectations, failure, and futility. He had refused to give up.[9]

It's so easy to get discouraged. There are so many voices telling us we can't do it. Others are better. We'll fail. We're not good enough. You've heard those voices. So have I. In fact, after having earned five degrees, hosting a national radio program, writing ten books, teaching at a major seminary, and enjoying a great marriage and family, I still hear those voices. But one of the many important messages of this book is that you *can* get it right after you've gotten it wrong. In fact, if you're willing to learn the lessons from failure, you're *more likely* to get it right after you've gotten it wrong.

Mike Singletary, former All-Pro linebacker for the Chicago Bears, was famous for the fact that when he initially got blocked out of a play, he would still make the tackle. What happened after he got knocked down on the first block? He got back up!

Several years ago, I heard Robert Schuller say, "Success is a matter of not quitting, and failure is a matter of giving up too soon!" That simple sentence made me stop and think. "Success is a matter of not quitting." There have been times in my life when I looked back and thought, *If only I had kept at it. If only I had tried one more time. Might I have succeeded?* Sometimes we've set unrealistic goals, or the events of life are such that the best choice is to quit. However, there are times when failure is caused by simply giving up too soon.

I've found that writing books is an emotional and sometimes painful process. This book has been no exception. In fact, there were several times when I had blocked out valuable time to write, but after a couple of hours, my computer screen was still blank. I wanted to quit. I felt discouraged, drained, and unable to type even one sentence. I felt like a failure. My mind was filled with a myriad of other "important" things I needed to do.

I decided to have a little talk with Jesus. I told Him, "Lord,

You've really gotten me into a fine mess this time! Remember, this book was Your idea. I wanted to write on something more comfortable and popular. Maybe something on relationships. Anything but failure. But no, You wouldn't have it. Every time Carrie and I prayed about a new writing project, this is what You put before us. You even brought us a publisher who had the courage to print it. Well, here I am, once again, sitting in front of a blank screen. Help!"

You can imagine that I was discouraged and more than a little frustrated. Then God gave me a great idea. He said, "Gary, why don't you put into practice what you're writing about?" I hadn't thought of that. I had fallen into the all-too-familiar trap of being so focused on the problem that I didn't see the solution. As I gave this project back to the Lord in prayer and sought the encouragement of my wife and friends, I was able to go back to my computer, sit down, and write. Each time, God was faithful. He met me, and the words flowed again.

9. God Can Bring Good Out of Bad

"And we know that in all things God works for the good of those who love Him, who have been called according to His purpose" (Rom. 8:28).

In 1928, Alexander Fleming made an uncharacteristically care-less mistake. He had completed his university and medical-school training and graduated with academic distinction. He served with honor in the army medical corps in World War I. Then he returned to research and teaching at the Royal College of Surgeons, trying to find antibacterial substances that would be nontoxic to animal tissues. He was a respected scientist who had achieved a measure of success.

While he was researching influenza in a dusty, old laboratory, a mold spore blew in through a window and contaminated a staphylococcus bacteria culture dish he was preparing to exam-ine. His seeming carelessness appeared to have ruined the culture.

But his response to that "mistake" resulted in what many

have called a triumph of accident and shrewd observation. Fleming noticed the mold had produced a bacteria-free spot in the previously thriving staphylococcus colony. Upon further investigation, he observed that the mold produced a substance that prevented staphylococcus growth, even when diluted eight hundred times. He named that substance penicillin, and medicine has not been the same since.

For his research, Fleming was knighted by the king, and in 1945 he shared the Nobel Prize. Because of Sir Alexander Fleming's mistake, hundreds of thousands of people have been healed and even saved from death.

Many of us become frantic over the fact of failure in our lives, and we'll go to all lengths in trying to hide it or rationalize about it. And all the time we're resisting one of God's most powerful instruments for conforming us to the likeness of our Lord Jesus Christ! "Failure where self is concerned in our Christian life and service, is allowed and often engineered by God in order to turn us completely from ourselves unto His Source for our life—Christ Jesus, who never fails."[10]

What I'm emphasizing here is not what we *do* but how we *think*. In a sense, surviving failure is the easy part. Learning from it in a way that changes us is the work. Failures come and failures go. But if in the process we can learn how to think more clearly about failure, if we'll take the time to listen for God's voice and look for His footprints in the failure, if we can remember that we *always* have choices, we'll have acquired an invaluable lesson that will help us the rest of our lives.

10. Maturity Doesn't Just Happen

"For whom He foreknew, He also predestined to become conformed to the image of His Son" (Rom. 8:29a, NASB).

We live in an age of instant everything. With the advent of credit cards, we don't have to wait for anything. We can have it all now. We may end up spending the rest of our lives paying for it, but it's ours for the charging.

Maturity doesn't work that way. In the Christian life, there's no such thing as quickie quality or microwave maturity. Most of us have a hard time understanding that God isn't in a hurry. He doesn't rush the development of our Christian life. When we're first saved, it's common to experience a period of rapid growth. God knows we need to develop a strong root system. But that doesn't continue. God also knows that if there's to be healthy development, the pace must be modified.

A.H. Strong tells the story of a student who asked the president of his school whether he couldn't take a shorter course than the one prescribed. "Oh yes," replied the president, "but then it depends upon what you want to be. When God wants to make an oak, He takes an hundred years, but when He wants to make a squash, He takes six months." Dr. Strong also wisely noted that growth in the tree is not uniform. During a four-to-six-week period in May, June, and July, there's a period of rapid growth when woody fiber is deposited between the bark and the trunk. There may be more growth during that short time than in the rest of the year combined. However, it's during the remainder of the year that solidification takes place. Without that process, the green timber would be useless.[11]

There's no shortcut to Christian maturity, either. God knows that true spiritual growth takes time and involves pain as well as joy, failure as well as success, suffering as well as happiness, and inactivity as well as service. If we understand Philippians 1:6, it will make things easier: "Being confident of this, that He who began a good work in you will carry it on to completion until the day of Christ Jesus."

Richard Foster has said it well:

If we fall down—and we *will* fall down—we get up and seek to obey again. We are forming the habit of obedience, and all habits begin with plenty of slips and falls and false starts. We did not learn to walk overnight. Or to play the piano. And we do not condemn ourselves unduly when we stub our toe or play a wrong note, do we? We must not condemn ourselves unduly in the spiritual life either. At first it will feel like we are doing the work, that we are the initiators. But in time we will see that it is God who inflames our heart with a burning craving for absolute purity.[12]

Small Beginnings

1. What are some of your responses that have kept you *behind* your failure?
2. What are some of your responses that have allowed you to grow *beyond* your failure?
3. Have you ever struggled to have a consistent quiet time with the Lord? What has helped you to succeed? What *hasn't* worked? This week, I would encourage you to do more of what God has shown you that works and less of what you already know doesn't work.
4. Over the past several months, what are some things God has tried to teach you through critics?

8. Overcoming Your Fear of Failure

In my mid-twenties, I learned the sport of rock climbing. It's fun, challenging, great exercise, and you get to see God's majesty and beauty from a unique and often precarious perspective. For years I had wanted to climb Devil's Tower. I'm sure you've seen pictures of this stump-shaped cluster of volcanic rock columns rising out of the plains of northeast Wyoming.

Finally my dream was about to come true. Three of us had spent months planning the climb, working with our gear, and checking out the routes. The day before our climb, we walked around the base of the tower, talked with the ranger, and got a last-minute weather report.

We woke the next morning to beautiful, clear skies, energetic and enthusiastic to begin our adventure. Step by step, hand over hand, we cautiously made our way up that enormous vertical wall of rock. By noon it was a pleasant 70 degrees, the sky was blue, and we were right on schedule. As the day went on, we noticed a few clouds passing overhead, but they were small and nothing to worry about. We continued our climb.

We were close to the top when suddenly a storm appeared over us. It had come over the tower from our blind side, so we had received no warning. The sky got dark. In less than an hour, the temperature dropped to the mid 40s. It began to rain, and then the rain turned into light hail. As we tried to continue our climb, we discovered that the rock became harder to hold onto. The vegetation that grew in various places became as slick as ice.

Finally we knew we had to stop. We were exhausted, cold, and more than a little scared. It didn't take long for fear to set in. A couple of us felt the muscles in our arms, hands, and fingers contract. One of the guys couldn't move his fingers, and he began to panic. The only way to the top was through a vertical route that was too slippery to navigate. The only way to the bottom was to rappel hundreds of feet down wet ropes and on slippery rock.

As we huddled, anchored together on a small ledge near the top of the rock, our fear alerted us to the danger of the situation. It gave us the energy and presence of mind to stop, catch our breath, assess our situation, and discuss our strategy. We helped our friend work through his panic, reviewed our plan, and slowly and carefully descended.

After a descent that took what seemed like hours, we made it safely to the bottom. We kissed the wonderful earth beneath our feet. We were bruised and emotionally drained, but we were on the ground and in one piece. Our God-given emotion of fear had served us well.

What Is Fear?

Fear is an unpleasant and often strong feeling caused by the anticipation or awareness of threat or danger. *Fear* comes from the Old English *faer*, which means sudden calamity or danger. It suggests a state of alarm or dread that, if strong enough, can immobilize us. When we experience fear, we're confronted with our limitations and vulnerability.

Normal, healthy fear serves an invaluable protective function. It warns us to keep away from dangerous people, places, or things. It can be essential in a time of crisis. God gave us the emotion of fear to provide us with energy and serve as a reminder to take our time, think through what we're doing, not panic, and act. When we understand fear and allow it to function in ways He has designed, it will serve us well, as on my climb on Devil's Tower.

Fear can also be experienced in unhealthy ways. When we allow our fears to control us, we tend to rehearse in our minds all the terrible things that could happen. We end up wasting our much-needed energy fighting imaginary problems rather than becoming effective in the here and now. We try to cross our bridges before we come to them and assume they're all going to break while we're in the middle.

Unhealthy fear tends to make us impatient, causing us to want to take things into our own hands. Fear magnifies our problems and then distorts our perspective so we can't think logically or clearly about them. Then it tends to paralyze us and hinder us from taking constructive action. The energy we've wasted on our fear cannot be used to help us solve the legitimate problem that first attracted our concern.

Fear also makes us more critical and causes us to feel threatened more easily and take offense at something that hasn't even happened. When we don't deal with our fears in the early stages, we become more vulnerable to worry, depression, and anger. Things go from bad to worse.

Fears out of control can become phobias. *Phobia* comes from the Greek word *phobos,* meaning "flight." It's derived from the deity of the same name who provoked panic and fear in his enemies. A phobia is a persistent fear of a person, object, or idea that clearly doesn't justify fear. A part of the phobic person knows the fear is absurd, but no amount of effort seems to overcome it.

Some of our fears have big names. A person can have a fear of lightning (astrophobia), bees (melissophobia), darkness (nycotophobia), or flying in an airplane (aviaphobia). If a friend cringes when he hears loud claps of thunder rumbling across a darkening sky, he suffers from brontophobia; if she just can't stand snakes, she struggles with ophidiophobia.

However, there's one kind of phobia you won't find in any psychiatric diagnostic manual. Yet it can have a more devastating effect than all the others combined. It can immobilize us, distort our perspective, rob us of our joy, keep us prisoners of our past, and limit our effectiveness for Christ. I refer to the fear of failure.

Why Is Fear of Failure Such a Problem?

I don't remember when I learned to fear failure. I don't think I learned it from my parents, but it must have been at an early age. I knew it was wrong to cheat, steal, or tell a lie. Those things were clearly sin, and I knew it was always wrong to sin. But somewhere along the way, I learned that making mistakes and falling short was almost as bad as sin. Clearly, it was something to be avoided.

Actually, it was more than to be avoided; it was something to be concealed or blamed on someone else. I see the same tendency in my children and in almost every person I've ever met.

Why do most people fear failure? Better yet, why do *you* fear failure? What are your first memories of it? How did you respond? How did those around you respond? Were you shamed? Were you punished? Were love and affection withheld? Did the way people respond leave you feeling hopeful or hopeless?

Somewhere in elementary school, I learned never to raise my hand unless I was sure I had the correct answer. Why? The teacher might embarrass me. I might look bad. My friends might make fun of me or, worse yet, they might not want to be around me. Embarrassment and rejection are powerful motivators.

One of the classic examples of the fear of failure involves the Children of Israel. In Numbers 13, God had delivered them from slavery to Pharaoh, parted the Red Sea, given them the Ten Commandments, provided for them, and protected them in their wilderness journey. Now they had come to the edge of the

Promised Land. God commanded them to send in twelve spies to survey the area. In verse 26, the spies brought back the report that the land was just as God had said it would be — flowing with milk and honey. So far, so good.

But if you look at the first word of the next verse, you'll see it starts with the word *Nevertheless*. In addition to their *confirmation* of God's description, they made an *observation*. Ten of the twelve spies had some grave concerns: There were large, walled, highly fortified cities, and some of the people were big and strong.

Still, one of the spies, Caleb, maintained a faith focus. He said, "Let's go for it. We can do it." He knew God's promises. He knew God's character. He kept his focus on what he knew to be true rather than allow himself to be sidetracked by the negative "what ifs."

It's too bad the rest of Israel didn't follow his lead. Instead, they took their eyes off God and focused on the negative possibilities. They didn't just cast a glance at the possible problems; they started staring at them. They chose to interpret them negatively. They moved from confirmation and observation to a *negative interpretation*.

The failure-focused spies told the people, "We can't attack those people; they are stronger than we are" (Num. 13:31b). Obviously, when they used the word *we*, they were totally forgetting about God. This was the same God who in Exodus 23:20-33 and 33:1-2 had told them this was the land He would give them. This was the same God who had brought the plagues on Pharaoh, parted the Red Sea, destroyed the mighty Egyptian army, and protected and provided for them in the wilderness. But they went from a faith focus to a failure focus.

If you look at verse 32b, you'll find that it didn't take long for a negative interpretation to lead to *exaggeration*. Not only did this land have walled cities and large people, but now the spies reported that the land "devours those living in it. All the people we saw there are of great size."

Their fear of failure, negative interpretation, and exaggerations spilled over to the Children of Israel. The confident and hopeful voices of Joshua and Caleb were drowned out by the anxious and fearful voices of the ten other spies.

By this time, the people had become paralyzed by their fear, and the decision had already been made. They were not going in. Who knew what horrible things might happen to them? The spies' distortions led to discouragement, which led to even greater distortions. In verse 33b, we read, "We seemed like grasshoppers in our own eyes, and we looked the same to them."

They were victims of the Grasshopper Complex, which is the result of having a failure focus. It occurs when we choose to look at our needs and concerns only in light of who we are and not in light of who God is and who we are in Him. It happens when we try to live life on our own; when we try to fight the battles in our own strength. When we lose perspective, our problems appear bigger than they really are . . . and we appear smaller.

Now, if the story were to end there, it would be bad enough. But it doesn't. It gets even more depressing. As we move into Numbers 14, we read that the people started to whine and weep. Their fear of failure increased their worry and led them into a deep depression. That can happen to us too. The more we focus on the negative, dwell on our problems, and allow ourselves to wander in the land of the negative "what ifs," the worse things will get.

In verse 3, we find that these folks got so out of touch with reality that they wanted to go back to Egypt. They totally forgot how hopeless and helpless they were in slavery. Later in that same chapter, we find that because of their lack of faith, they were forced to wander in the wilderness for forty years. They had seen God's power, His glory, His signs, and His faithfulness, yet they still chose to test Him (see Num. 14:22).

Because they chose to be fearful rather than faithful, only two of the adult males who had left Egypt, Joshua and Caleb, were allowed to see the Promised Land. Over the next forty years, the approximately 600,000 other males died. That's roughly one funeral every 20 minutes, 24 hours a day, for 40 years. Now, *that's* depressing! Their grave but misplaced concerns led them to their graves rather than to the grace and goodness God had prepared for them in the Promised Land.

Before I go further, let's look at a summary of some of the differences between having a failure focus and a faith focus:

Failure Focus	*Faith Focus*
looks at problem	looks for the solution
looks at fear	looks through the fear
manna	milk and honey
sees the obstacle	sees the opportunity
assumes the worst	assumes the best
restrains (limits) God	releases God
past determines present	God's promises determine the present
short-term thinking	long-term thinking
time-limited perspective	eternal perspective
go back to Egypt	go into the Promised Land
results in stagnation	results in sanctification

As you read this chapter, you may be facing your own private "Canaan." As you look around you, there may be "walls" of difficulty and "giants" of discouragement. As you look at the weeks and months ahead, you may not be able to see how you'll survive.

In such times, it's tempting to fall into the same trap as the Children of Israel — to listen to the critics, take your eyes off God, and become consumed by your problems. It's easy to allow your legitimate concern to give in to fear, to play it safe and do nothing. But ultimate failure comes when you fail to try, not when you try and fail. Playing it safe and doing nothing will only make things worse.

Theodore Roosevelt had a great philosophy about confronting criticism and risking failure:

It's not the critic who counts; not the man who points out how the strong man stumbled or where the doer of deeds could have done them better. The credit belongs to the man who is actually in the arena; whose face is marred by dust and sweat and blood; who strives valiantly; who errs, and comes short again and again, because there is not effort without error and shortcoming; who does actually try to do the deed; who knows the great enthusiasm, the great devotion, and spends himself in a worthy cause; who, at the worst, if he fails, at least fails while daring greatly. Far better it is to dare mighty things, to win glorious triumphs even though checkered by failure, than to rank with those poor spirits who neither enjoy nor suffer much because they live in the gray twilight that knows neither victory nor defeat.[1]

My experience has been that in difficult times, it's not the size of your giants that counts but the size of your God. It's who *He* is; it's how you've seen *Him* work in the past; it's what *He* has promised.

God said we're more than conquerors, not more than survivors. The price of being captive to the fear of failure is too high for any of us to pay. The more we feed our fear of failure, the worse it becomes. We limit God, quench the Holy Spirit, and condemn ourselves to a life of mediocrity.

As I've noted in earlier chapters, we can grow and learn from losing as well as from winning. Our desire to learn can be motivated by our desire to overcome failure and frustration. If we take the time to analyze why we failed, we can learn from our mistakes, correct our errors, and do something different in the future.

Losing once in a while also makes us more human. It ensures a feeling of humility. It makes us aware of our limitations and demonstrates how we're dependent on others for what we lack ourselves. It can give us a sensitivity and compassion that make others around us feel safe, understood, and needed.

Remember what Paul said in 2 Corinthians 3:4-5: "Such confidence as this is ours through Christ before God. Not that we are competent in ourselves to claim anything for ourselves, but our competence comes from God." Remember when you're discouraged and disappointed, "But as for me, I watch in hope for the Lord, I wait for God my Savior; my God will hear me. Do not gloat over me, my enemy! Though I have fallen, I will rise. Though I sit in darkness, the Lord will be my light" (Micah 7:7-8).

You Can Overcome Your Fear of Failure

Jim grew up in a home where he never saw his parents fail. And they never gave him permission to fail, either. "I've spent forty-two years of my life playing it safe," he told me. "I've stayed out of trouble. I've hid from anything that might expose my feelings of inadequacy and inferiority."

At an early age, he learned there was no such thing as unconditional love. Enough was never enough. Smiles, touches, hugs, praise, and encouragement were reserved for success and achievement. "Somewhere in my teenage years, I put my life on cruise control and went into hiding," he said. He learned to read people, anticipate rejection, fear conflict, avoid criticism, and hide behind the mask of whatever he thought people wanted him to be.

Jim continued, "My parents weren't bad people. They loved me, they loved the Lord, they took me to church, and they provided for all my physical needs. But somewhere along the way, I learned that love was conditional. If I didn't perform, if I didn't get it right, or if I made them look bad, I was treated as if I didn't exist."

When I asked Jim what had led him to make an appointment with me, his response was immediate: "I feel like life is passing me by. I'm not happy, and I know God's not pleased with me. I don't know myself. I don't respect myself. Apart from being a good provider, I've been of limited spiritual value to my wife and kids." After a long pause, for the first time in that session he looked me straight in the eyes. "Dr. Oliver," he said, "I'm sick of being a nobody. I'm ready to become the man God would have me to be."

As you might imagine, Jim had a lot of fear of failure to overcome if he was going to reach his goal. I'm happy to say, however, that he has made significant progress and now feels much better about himself and his relationship with God. Let me show you the same steps I helped him work through in winning his victory.

The most important steps to overcoming your fear of failure must be taken *before* you're afraid. If you're even semismart, you won't wait until the five minutes before a major exam to study for it; you won't start preparing for a marathon an hour before the race begins. Real change takes time. But there's no time like the present to begin.

Step 1. Look to God

If you have a failure focus, you're looking at the past and allowing it to shape your life. You're letting it tell you who you are and what you can do. Even more debilitating than that, you're allowing the past to tell you who *God* is and what *He* can do.

If you look at God instead, you'll develop a faith focus. That divine perspective will help you learn from the past, look at the present, and anticipate the future. You'll see yourself as a child of God who has been saved by grace and is becoming conformed to the image of His Son.

What are some of the things in your past that Satan has used to distort your perspective and discourage and defeat you? What are some of the things that have had a strong limiting influence, robbed you of joy, kept you from trying again, and led you to play it safe rather than take a chance and step out in faith? What are some of the events you have blamed for your inability to grow? Here are some of the most common things I've seen:

handicaps	troubled family background
past failures	shame over some personal/ family "secret"
pride	too much success
painful experiences	innocent mistakes
fame	recognition
shame	excessive wealth
guilt	bad luck

While Jim loved the Lord, led a moral life, and was active in his church, he was consumed with his weakness and inadequacies. But when we allow ourselves to be controlled by such fear of failure, we're assuming responsibility that God never intended us to have. Our identity has been determined by the God who created and redeemed us. It's not determined by our production or what others think or say about us. Therefore, as we approach the challenge of overcoming that paralyzing fear, we must start by fixing our eyes on Jesus Christ, "the author and perfecter of our faith" (Heb. 12:2). One preacher said it well:

Christ does not change. He is the same yesterday and today and forever. And the truth of His teaching doesn't change either. You can count on it, indeed. You can stake your life on it.

The most wonderful thing that can happen to any of us is to have that most profound of all experiences — to know Jesus Christ personally. You can hear about Him all your life and never really know Him. You can believe that He lived and respect Him and honor Him as a great historical figure and still only know Him academically.

But when at last you find Him and experience His reality, when for you He comes out of the stained-glass windows and out of history and becomes your personal Savior, then you can walk through all manner of darkness and pain and trouble and be unafraid.[2]

Step 2. Turn Back to the Bible

If you're at all like Jim, if you've spent even a small portion of your life struggling with the fear of failure, you know just how consuming that fear can become. What started as an awareness of the possibility of failure can quickly turn into a preoccupation. An absolutely essential part of overcoming the fear of failure is to "set your minds on things above, not on earthly things" (Col. 3:2). Here are a few verses you'll find helpful:

"Even though I walk through the valley of the shadow of death, I will fear no evil, for You are with me; Your rod and Your staff, they comfort me" (Ps. 23:4).

"God is our refuge and strength, an ever-present help in trouble. Therefore we will not fear, though the earth give way and the mountains fall into the heart of the sea, though its waters roar and foam and the mountains quake with their surging" (Ps. 46:1-3).

"Cast your cares on the Lord and He will sustain you; He will never let the righteous fall" (Ps. 55:22).

"Surely God is my salvation; I will trust and not be afraid" (Isa. 12:2).

"So do not fear, for I am with you; do not be dismayed, for I am your God. I will strengthen you and help you; I will uphold you with My righteous right hand" (Isa. 41:10).

"But He said to me, 'My grace is sufficient for you, for My power is made perfect in weakness.' . . . That is why, for Christ's sake, I delight in weaknesses, in insults, in hardships, in persecutions, in difficulties. For when I am weak, then I am strong" (2 Cor. 12:9-10).

Step 3. Ask God to Help You See Failure Through His Eyes

As we saw in chapter 4, God sees failure in a different light from our human tendencies. And He wants to teach us the power of Spirit-controlled failure. I can hear you asking yourself, "What in the world does Oliver mean by that?" Let me explain.

Several years ago, I heard about a professor at the University of Houston who had developed a unique course in creativity that his students nicknamed "Failure 101." Early in the course, he assigned tasks that helped his students desensitize their fear of failure. Over time, they learned how to equate failure with innovation instead of defeat. Gradually they became more willing to try new things.

One of the assignments was for each student to start a moneymaking business on campus by the end of the semester. Most students had at least five failures before finding their business niche. But all of them learned not to take failure personally. They learned how to learn from their failures. They also learned there are two kinds of failure.

They labeled the first kind "slow, stupid failure." That's where it takes a long time to maximize your mistakes. The people keep on doing the same thing over and over until one day the light comes on and they get the message, "This isn't working."

The students labeled the second kind "intelligent, fast failure." It occurs when you've learned how to learn from your mistakes. You might have already guessed that Spirit-controlled failure is intelligent, fast failure. Because of who we are in Christ and what God has promised in His Word, we don't have to fear failure. In God's hands, it can become our friend.

When I first talked with Jim about the possibility of harnessing the positive power of failure, he thought I was crazy. So I asked him to put together a list of three potential benefits of failure. He ended up with five of them, and I've added my own commentary to each one. Here they are:

1. "If Romans 8:28 and the other promises of God's Word are true, then He can use my failures." The turning point for Jim came when he started to look at what he thought and felt in light of the clear teaching of Scripture. He was amazed at what he found.

2. "Failure can give me an opportunity to learn." This is why many MBA programs have their students study unsuccessful

companies. Success is enjoyable, but it doesn't teach the same things we can learn from failure.

3. "Failure gives me new options." The one area of study that knows the value of failure is science. Most of the great breakthroughs came only after hundreds of failures. In my experience, the people who are the most successful in coping with failure are those who have learned how to define failure as new data, new information to learn from, who concentrate on the process of what they can learn and not the product of their error.

4. "Failure provides an opportunity for growth." If you've read this far in the book, you know that a certain amount of failure is necessary for growth. While too much failure can overwhelm and demoralize, too much success can make an individual cocky and complacent. The ability to change and make progress is an integral part of growing. It involves the capacity to profit from our mistakes and to overcome obstacles and failures. Without failure and frustration, we would stagnate.

5. "You can't always prevent failure because you can't control all the variables. However, you can control the effects of failure; you can choose what failure will do to you or for you." Jim had spent most of his life like a billiard ball, being pushed around by the cue ball of circumstances. As he began to grasp the power of this insight, he was able to move from being merely reactive to being more proactive.

Step 4. Maintain a Sense of Humor

At the beginning of one of our sessions, Jim announced that he had a story to tell me. He wasn't exactly the story-telling kind of guy, so I listened with interest. It turned out to be a funny story, and as Jim told it, he laughed.

Laughter is good. It's important to cultivate a good sense of humor, especially if you tend to be a perfectionist. With a smile on your face, you can see some additional advantages in losing. One of the biggest is that it puts you among a lot of friends. Besides that, losers make it possible for winners to win, so all winners owe a great deal to losers.

Another advantage of failure is that you can be much more creative and rebellious. Winners need to play by the rules. They need to employ advanced and sophisticated strategies. But losers are free to do whatever they want. I've interviewed numerous individuals who have found losing to be more interesting, challenging, and enjoyable than winning. For one thing, there are many more ways to lose.

One writer summarized the value of losing from the lighter side with this observation: "Victory is fragile and apt to break apart at any moment, whereas a losing streak can be maintained for an indefinite period without violation. And when that rare success does break through the clouds with a shattering glare, you savor forever the contrast of victory gained through stubborn, imaginative failure."[3]

Step 5. Admit Your Fear

When you find yourself face-to-face with your fear, what's the first thing you should do? What have you done in the past? Assume the worst, replay past failures, review all your shortcomings, run and hide? Have any of those responses helped? If not, try a new approach.

Start by admitting you're afraid. Sometimes this is easier said than done. But all it involves is saying, "I'm afraid." At this point, you don't need to know why you're afraid. Just saying it will give you a tremendous sense of freedom and victory in having the strength and courage to admit it.

Once you've admitted your fear, the next step is to identify it. Simply ask yourself, *What am I afraid of?* Jim found it helpful to journal his fears, where he recorded the following: (1) When I experience the fear, is there a pattern? (2) How long does the fear last? (3) How intense is it? and (4) What am I aware of being afraid of?

As you look at the list, ask yourself, *Are these fears healthy or unhealthy? Are they rational or irrational? Are they coming from a failure focus or a faith focus? Are there any promises in God's*

Word that relate to my fear? How have I responded in the past that hasn't worked? What can I do differently?

This step is a lot like fighting the childhood fear of the ghost in the closet. The longer you lie in bed and think about it, listen for it, imagine how big and strong and angry it is, the more your fear grows. But if you reach over, grab a flashlight, and look in the closet, you'll discover there's no ghost.

Step 6. Face Your Fears

Now it's time to ask the big question: "Can I decrease and even eliminate my fear?" The great news is you can. The bad news is that the solution always involves gradually facing your fears. There's no need to rush into it, however. You can take your time.

There have been occasions in my Christian life when I've struggled with what seemed like an absolute conflict between the reality of a biblical truth and the reality of my experience. For example, the Bible says that "my God will meet all your needs according to His glorious riches in Christ Jesus" (Phil. 4:19). However, there've been many times when I thought my needs weren't being supplied. The Bible says that "we are more than conquerors" (Rom. 8:37), but there've been many times when I've felt like anything *but* a conqueror.

There's a word for this kind of experience. It's called *dissonance*. The *American Heritage Dictionary* defines it as "a harsh, disagreeable combination of sounds; discord: lack of agreement, consistency, or harmony; conflict." In music, it's when two tones don't blend but instead cause you to cover your ears and duck for cover. Musical dissonance is resolved when the conflicting sounds merge into a harmonious chord. When ideas or thoughts collide, psychologists call it *cognitive dissonance.*

Have you ever experienced a gap—even a chasm—between what you understood God's Word to say about what you should be experiencing and what you were actually going through? Jim had lived his entire life with a growing dissonance between what he taught, what he believed, and how he lived. As he learned to apply the truth of God's Word to his real-life situation, however, he was surprised at how quickly the dissonance decreased.

Any time you come to "Canaans" in your life, you'll come face-to-face with what appear to be unbeatable giants. But don't do what the ten Israelite spies did. Don't do what the Children of Israel did. There's a much better option. The way that worked for Jim (and has worked for literally hundreds of others) is to open your journal and make a list of your ten worst fears. Then rank them in order of the power they have over you, with your greatest fear at number one and your smallest at number ten.

Now start with number ten. On Jim's list, that was fear of being criticized by coworkers. As we discussed some possible solutions, he decided that, rather than wait for someone to criticize him, he would be proactive and ask people for specific suggestions on how he could improve.

Next, he identified three individuals at work who were fairly nonthreatening, and over a two-week period, he asked each of them, "If there was one area of my life that I could change that would help me be a better coworker, what would it be?"

The first time he did it was the hardest. But he was surprised at how much easier it became. He was also surprised to find that, while each of his coworkers made a suggestion for how he could improve, they all offered several compliments as well for what they saw as his many strengths. If he hadn't been open to criticism, he probably would never have heard those praises.

While Jim experienced some fairly dramatic progress in a short time, don't forget that it takes real courage to press on in the face of what seems to be certain failure. For the short term, it's easier to live with the only true failure — never trying. Staying where we are is at least familiar and nonthreatening. It feels more secure. Unfortunately, the security we feel is false. That short-lived sense of safety will eventually give way to the stench of stagnation. Risking potential failure can be scary. But living in the fear of failure is tragic.

Step 7. Mine the Experience All You Can

For many people, failure is like a deep, dark mine shaft. It's not fun to go into it. It may trigger other fears. But that's where the gold is. And if you want the gold, sometimes you have to be willing to get down and dirty and dig for it.

There's also gold in the dark hills of our failures. Sometimes it's visible at the surface, and sometimes we have to dig deep for it. Because of the pain that failure involves, most people only scrape the surface gold and rarely hit the mother lode of opportunity and insight. But when you run out of easy answers, make the time to dig a bit deeper. Look for the new growth point. If you're committed to becoming the person God wants you to be, you won't have to stay stuck for very long. In the excitement, humility, and gratitude of growth, you'll discover failure will provide for the renewal that will help you sustain true success.

As I was growing up in Southern California, the USC Trojans were my favorite football team. One All-American who had enjoyed the glory years at USC was drafted by the Tampa Bay Buccaneers, one of the worst teams in the National Football League. They were so bad and lost so many games that they became the most feared team in professional football — everybody was afraid of the humiliation of being the first team to lose to them.

After surviving a disastrous season in which the team lost every game, that former USC star said, "This has been very difficult for me. Winning has been part of my life. I will never adjust to losing. Losing has affected my personal life. Football shouldn't be that important, but to me it is . . . winning made life enjoyable. You wanted to go out, have a good time. Winning made you happy. Now, I not only do not want to go out, I don't even enjoy eating. And I can't sleep."[4]

Another outstanding football player had a different response to failure, however. He was the quarterback on a team that had lost three games after being ranked number one in the country. He was interviewed after bouncing back with a decisive win.

"Losing is a growing experience," he said. "Because of last year, we fell into the trap of thinking we'd never lose again. But we found out that wasn't to be. Losing brought us down to earth, made us more determined, and made us work harder."[5]

Through many ups and downs, the Apostle Paul learned how to look at pain and failures as messengers from God. And that's been my experience. Some of the greatest lessons I've learned—some of the biggest blessings I've received—have been the fruit of mistakes and failures.

The distinguishing feature of mature people is this: They've not only overcome their fear of failure, but they've also learned how to learn from their failure. You can learn to overcome your fear of failure. I did. Jim did. But remember that it starts with step 1; it starts with looking to God:

But whatever was to my profit I now consider loss for the sake of Christ. What is more, I consider everything a loss compared to the surpassing greatness of knowing Christ Jesus my Lord, for whose sake I have lost all things. I consider them rubbish, that I may gain Christ and be found in Him, not having a righteousness of my own that comes from the Law, but that which is through faith in Christ—the righteousness that comes from God and is by faith. I want to know Christ and the power of His resurrection and the fellowship of sharing in His sufferings, becoming like Him in His death, and so, somehow, to attain to the resurrection from the dead.

Not that I have already obtained all this, or have already been made perfect, but I press on to take hold of that for which Christ Jesus took hold of me. Brothers, I do not consider myself yet to have taken hold of it. But one thing I do: Forgetting what is behind and straining toward what is ahead, I press on toward the goal to win the prize for which God has called me heavenward in Christ Jesus (Phil. 3:7-14).

Small Beginnings
1. What are some of the fears you struggle with today?
2. To what extent do you have a fear of failure?
3. Summarize in one sentence what it means to have a failure focus, and in another what it means to have a faith focus.
4. What is one specific way you can apply 2 Corinthians 3:4-5 in your life this week?

9. Overcoming Moral and Sexual Failure

I'll never forget the time I saw my first piece of pornography. I was an eighth-grader at Hill Junior High. I was sitting in the library, working on a reading assignment, when my friend Carl came over and sat down next to me. He looked around and, in a very low voice, asked if I wanted to see something.

I was curious. The tone of his voice and the way he was acting suggested it was probably something I shouldn't see. Of course, that made me even more curious. After only a few seconds of contemplation, I said, "Sure!" He looked around once more and pulled out a folder.

When he opened the folder, there was a "girlie" magazine. I had heard about them, but I'd never seen one. Until that time, the only female nudity I had seen had been in *National Geographic.* While I had found those photos interesting, this was much more exciting. He told me his dad had a bunch of these at home and that he would sell me this copy for fifty cents. I didn't even have to think about it. I handed over two quarters, and it was mine.

I knew that what I was doing was wrong. I knew it displeased God. But I was able to rationalize it. It wasn't that bad. Besides, it wasn't as if I were lying, cheating, or stealing. Those things are clearly sin. Nowhere does the Bible say, "Thou shalt not look at pornography." This was just a harmless magazine.

But it wasn't harmless. What happened that day fueled what was to become a lifelong struggle with lust, sensuality, and impurity. It followed me into high school, through college and seminary, and at times even into the present. Most of the time, I've had victory over these temptations. But there have been times when I haven't, times when I allowed the thought of a quick and "harmless" thrill to become overwhelming. And without exception, each time the promised pleasure has been engulfed by guilt, shame, and sorrow.

Now, please don't misunderstand me. I'm not blaming that single exposure to pornography for all the sins of my single years or the struggles I've had as a married man. But I do know that when the normal God-given desire that has been damaged and distorted by sin is exposed to abnormal and immoral stimulation, there's going to be trouble. It's amazing how quickly a sincere and deep desire for purity and a determination to do what's right can disappear. And this is a struggle faced by both men and women.

Sharon became a Christian as a junior in college. After her conversion, she got involved in a campus ministry as well as a local, Bible-teaching church, and was discipled by the woman who had led her to the Lord.

Early in her senior year, she met a dynamic young man named Warren who was a senior at a local Christian college. "Warren seemed to have everything on my list, starting with a love for the Lord and a desire to serve Him," Sharon said. "We fell in love and were married the summer of our graduation."

Before long, Sharon was pregnant, and within the next few years, she and Warren would become the parents of three young children. By the time she came to see me, she was in her early thirties—and scared to death because she had allowed herself to become emotionally involved with the husband of one of her best friends.

In a voice that quivered with anxiety, she told me, "I don't know how this happened. I love the Lord, I love Warren, and I love my family. I want my marriage to work." And then she added emphatically, "But I don't want it to continue the way it has been."

She went on to tell an all-too-common story of a woman whose husband had allowed himself to become so consumed with providing for his family that he failed to provide his wife (and himself) with the kinds of things God designed the marriage relationship to give us. As he became busier at work and their preschoolers demanded every ounce of Sharon's strength, they drifted apart.

A friend of hers loaned her a romance novel, and "I found myself captivated by the intrigue, love, and romance that was there," she said. The more she read, the more dissatisfied she became with her own marriage. "I began to see only Warren's faults," she said. "The more I focused on my unmet needs, the more they seemed to grow." And the more she began to fantasize about the possibility of someone else meeting them.

Sharon and Warren had been in a Bible study with Tom and Anna for only a couple of months when Sharon became aware of a mutual attraction. She sensed a tenderness and sensitivity in Tom that she hadn't experienced from Warren in years. "It wasn't long," she said, "before I would visualize myself in stories I read and see Tom as the perfect man who would meet all my needs and fulfill all my dreams."

When she finally realized what was going on, "I was afraid and ashamed. I couldn't believe this could happen to me." Fortunately, Sharon listened to the convicting voice of the Holy Spirit, received some wise counsel from an older woman in their church, and told Warren what had been going on. While he was shocked, he was also convicted about his role in their drifting apart. It was he who suggested they go for marriage counseling to rebuild their relationship.

At the end of their first session with me, Sharon shook her head and said, "I always thought it was just men who struggle with moral purity, that it was men who had the wandering eyes and wandering hearts and were unfaithful." But as her story shows, that's not the case; both men and women are vulnerable to temptation.

A Culture in Moral Decline

The struggle with moral purity is made especially difficult by the fact that we're surrounded by a culture that no longer believes in any absolute moral standard. A lot of people today, including professionals who ought to know better, would have told Sharon there was nothing wrong with her fantasies about Tom. Even if she had decided to leave Warren to pursue a physical relationship with Tom, many would have cheered her on. Those same people would tell me to go ahead and enjoy pornography whenever I got the urge.

How and when did this moral decline get started? Although it's impossible to pin down the cause to any one person or event, a book published in 1966 proved to be extremely influential. The author was an American professor named Joseph Fletcher, and the book was called *Situation Ethics*. Fletcher's basic premise was that nothing is universally good or bad, right or wrong. There are no absolutes. Morals are determined by the situation. An act that may be wrong in one situation (like adultery) may be right in another.

What in 1966 was only a philosophical discussion has in 1995 become the amoral foundation of our society. Thirty-five years ago, our country followed the Judeo-Christian ethic. Few people questioned that premarital chastity was a good thing, that hard work was the duty of any responsible person, that homosexual conduct was wrong, and that it was never right to lie, cheat, steal, or commit adultery. But the tragic truth is that today, our ethics and morals are no longer based on Jerusalem. Instead, they're based on Sodom and Gomorrah.

It's easy to talk about how hard it is to live a pure life. It's tempting to bemoan what we can't change and ignore what we can. It's much more comfortable to focus on the breakdown of the corporate morality of our society than to allow the Holy Spirit to make us aware of our own moral failures. It's less threatening to discuss the very real evils of pornography and sexual addiction than the sin of gossip. It's easier to discuss the shocking lyrics of some contemporary music than the sin of gluttony.

While there's a lot we can't change, there are clearly some things that we can. If we dwell on the influences that are beyond our control, we'll become frustrated and discouraged. But as we focus on the influences we can control, we *can* become hopeful. We have to be willing to allow God to show us our contribution to the problem, which will then lead us to our part in the solution.

In Romans 14, Paul talked about how easy it is to pass judgment on the weaknesses of others. But in verse 12, he reminded us that "each of us will give an account of himself to God." What are some small steps we can take to be part of the solution? If you've read this far, you've already taken the first step, which is to be aware of the problem. As someone once said, "A problem defined is a problem half solved."

But there's more. Ask yourself, *In what areas am I the weakest? In what areas am I most easily tempted to compromise? What aspects of my life reveal the greatest inconsistencies?* I've found that one of the easiest ways to identify my own potential blind spots is to look at which attitudes or behaviors I'm most likely to minimize or excuse.

If we truly want to be people whose lives are characterized by moral and ethical purity, we must take steps to put that resolve into practice. Aristotle wrote that virtue involves not only *knowing* what's right, but also *choosing to do* what's right. And we need to make that choice consistently and repeatedly until it becomes a habit.

To help you in keeping your commitment to moral purity, the rest of this chapter offers six keys that I've found essential in keeping my own.

Key 1: Make a Decision

I lived through the trauma and tragedy of the Watergate scandal. Recently the British Broadcasting Corporation produced a five-hour documentary on this event that rocked our nation, caused a president to resign, and changed the face of American politics. One of the programs replayed a part of Richard Nixon's 1977 interview with David Frost.

"I fouled up," Nixon said, "in the arena where I'm supposed to be a master . . . politics." As I watched that interview in the context of the entire Watergate scandal, I realized Nixon was wrong. The cause of his downfall wasn't his failure in the arena of politics. It was his failure and the corporate failure of "all the president's men" in the arena of morality and ethics. The cancer of corruption started with what probably seemed like a series of small compromises. The morality of the end was used to justify the immorality of the means.

It's not easy to be pure in an impure world. Even if you become a cultural ostrich and avoid all movies, listen only to Christian radio, and read only Christian books and magazines, you're still going to struggle. You'll never become godly by negation, by merely avoiding everything. A pure, pollution-free environment doesn't make pure people. According to Mark 7:15 and 20-23, it's what's *inside* that defiles a person.

A fresh start begins with a fresh end. Many people want to have a new beginning, but they fail to bury and cover with dirt the past patterns of thinking, feeling, and choosing. Is there something you need to let go of? Is there a habit you're tempted to rationalize? Is there an activity that, while it's not sin, is clearly leading you *away from* rather than *closer to* Christ?

I remember singing, as a young child, a hymn called "Dare to Be a Daniel." The chorus said, "Dare to be a Daniel, dare to stand alone! Dare to have a purpose firm! Dare to make it known!"[1] Today God is looking for men and women who have the courage to become twentieth-century Daniels. And it all starts with a choice to remain pure whatever the cost.

Key 2: Learn How to Deal with Temptation by Being Offensive

Temptations can serve a useful function in our lives even though they seem to cause us nothing but pain. God allows them to keep us humble and alert, and to instruct us. He can use them to reveal our selfishness, our pride, our instability, and our lack of trust in Him.

One of the main reasons God allows temptations is to reveal who we are and where He wants to help us grow. That's why it's important for us to pay attention to them. The Bible is clear that the best response to temptation is to "flee the evil desires of youth" (2 Tim. 2:22). That's a good start. But the answer to defeating temptations isn't just running away.

As I look back at my own life, I see a pattern that's confirmed in the experience of hundreds of men and women with whom I've worked. When my *only* response to temptation was to run away, when I didn't deal with the core weakness and vulnerability that God was allowing the temptation to reveal, I made little progress in my Christian life. I would be fine for a while. But it was like trying to control a yard full of weeds by only pulling off the top of the weed. Eventually the lion of lust would start to roar, and over time the temptations returned more quickly and with greater power.

After much trial and error (I'm a slow learner), I discovered that I was more successful in dealing with temptations if I caught them at the very beginning and dealt with the roots. Temptations are much easier to overcome if we meet them at the door and say "No, thank you" than if we allow them to enter our minds.

In his devotional classic *The Imitation of Christ*, Thomas à Kempis wrote that "we should not strive for a peace that is without temptation, or for a life that never feels adversity. Peace is not found by escaping temptations, but by being tried by them. We will have discovered peace when we have been tried and come through the trial of temptation."[2]

In dealing with temptation, the best defense is a good offense. Get serious about it. Determine when and where you're the weakest, and develop a plan to deal with it. I've discovered that one of Satan's favorite places to tempt me is when I'm on the road in a hotel room. The TV is there, the remote is there, and the destructive programming is there.

To deal with that, when I travel, I take a picture of my family and put it on top of the TV. I open my Bible and put it on the dresser next to the TV. I call home every night to talk and pray with my wife and kids. Sometimes I take a small cassette player and listen to praise music. Each of these "little things" is a powerful reminder of who God has called me to be.

You'll have to decide what works for you. Some men phone the front desk and ask them to shut off the adult movie channel. I've worked with other men who found it helpful to put the remote where they wouldn't be tempted to pick it up. It isn't a sin to go channel surfing, but most of the men I've worked with who struggle with impurity have told me that spending hours watching pornographic movies in the privacy of their room started with that seemingly innocent activity.

When you first hear the soft and seductive voice of temptation, fight it. Don't analyze it or rationalize it. Run if necessary (and it is almost always necessary)! What you do in the first sixty seconds after you've been tempted will determine the outcome; the battle is won or lost in the first minute.

Don't excuse your small, minor blind spot in light of all the sacrifices you're making, all the work you're doing, all the things that God is accomplishing through you. Open your Bible and read the second half of 2 Timothy 2:22: "And pursue righteousness, faith, love and peace, along with those who call on the Lord out of a pure heart."

Our Heroes
by Phoebe Cary

Here's a hand to the boy who has courage
To do what he knows to be right;

When he falls in the way of temptation,
He has a hard battle to fight.
Who strives against self and his comrades
Will find a most powerful foe.
All honor to him if he conquers.
A cheer for the boy who says "NO!"
There's many a battle fought daily
The world knows nothing about;
There's many a brave little soldier
Whose strength puts a legion to rout.
And he who fights sin singlehanded
Is more of a hero, I say,
Than he who leads soldiers to battle
And conquers by arms in the fray.
Be steadfast, my boy, when you're tempted,
To do what you know to be right,
Stand firm by the colors of manhood
And you will o'ercome in the fight.
"The right," be your battle cry ever
In waging the warfare of life,
And God, who knows who are the heroes,
Will give you the strength for the strife.[3]

Key 3: Determine Where the Line Is, and Stay a Safe Distance Away

Most Christians want to be strong and victorious. At the end of our lives, we want to hear God say, "Well done, thou good and faithful servant." We want our lives to be characterized by integrity. The problem is that each of us has blind spots, weaknesses, and deeply entrenched habits that can sabotage our best intentions and take us over the line into moral or ethical failure.

The remedy for this is to stop thinking in terms of how much we can get away with and still not sin and determine instead what kinds of things are healthy and which are unhealthy. *In other words, once we determine where the line of sin is in each area where we tend to be tempted, we need to walk ten yards back away from it and draw ourselves another line there — then make* that *the line we're careful not to cross.*

When I was a young Christian, I chose Philippians 1:20 as my life verse: "I eagerly expect and hope that I will in no way be ashamed, but will have sufficient courage so that now as always Christ will be exalted in my body, whether by life or by death." I'm sad to say that I've sometimes fallen short of that goal, but it has rarely been because I made a conscious decision to compromise or sin. More often it was because I allowed myself to spend too much time walking too close to the line.

Each of us needs to ask God to help us determine where the line is in those areas where we're most vulnerable. If it's not something that's clearly spelled out in Scripture, we should pray about it and seek the counsel of several wise friends. And again, once God has shown you where the line is, *always* leave yourself a margin. If God has told you not to go beyond the 50-yard line, don't tiptoe up to the 49-yard, 2-foot-and-11-inch mark. Don't see how close you can get without going over. That's about as smart as a scuba diver seeing how little air he can leave in his tank and still get to the surface. Only a fool would do something like that.

Key 4: Guard Your Heart

In April 1994, Aldrich Ames, a highly trusted, thirty-one-year CIA counterintelligence officer, pleaded guilty to giving up some of the CIA's most precious secrets. Ames, who was sentenced to life in prison with no chance of parole, said he had "betrayed a serious trust" but played down the damage caused by his nine years of work as a double agent.

Prosecutors, on the other hand, said he had caused the deaths, arrests, or disappearances of at least ten Russian and one East European double agents. They claimed he was motivated by greed alone in carrying out what officials described as the worst security breach in the forty-seven-year history of the CIA.

Aldrich Ames tried to serve two masters, and it didn't work. Christ made it clear that we *can't* serve two masters (see Matt. 6:24). Where our treasure is, there will our heart be also (see Matt. 6:21). Moral and ethical purity start in the heart. Only the passionate love of purity can save a person from impurity. That's why Proverbs tells us, "Above all else, guard your affections. For they influence everything else in your life." It goes on to warn us, "Spurn the careless kiss of a prostitute. Stay far from her. Look straight ahead; don't even turn your head to look. Watch your step. Stick to the path and be safe. Don't sidetrack; pull back your foot from danger" (Prov. 4:23-27, TLB).

Are there any prostitutes in your life? Hear me out before you answer. When most people think of a prostitute, they think of someone who sells herself for money. However, a prostitute can be any person, habit, or activity that promises short-term pleasure for a high price, that makes you forget the most important for the least important, that increases your vulnerability.

Let me ask the question a different way. Are there any thoughts, habits, possessions, or activities in your life that are more important to you than God, that make you more vulnerable to compromise and sin? If so, giving in to that is like giving in to the careless kiss of a prostitute. Proverbs warns us to stay as far away from these things as possible.

How do you do that? By looking for and focusing on all the potential pitfalls? No! The only solution is to set your mind on things above, to fix your eyes on Jesus. When Christ met Peter on the seashore after His resurrection, He didn't bawl him out for his lack of faith in denying Him. Three times He asked Peter the simple question, "Do you love Me?" A growing affection for our Lord Jesus Christ is the only antidote for the kind of apathy that leads down the primrose path to compromise.

Key 5: Gird Your Mind

Every moment of every day, a spiritual war is occurring in your life, and the battlefield is your mind. An important part of what it means to be made in God's image is that you have a mind, your seat of reflective consciousness. It performs activities such as perceiving, problem-solving, remembering, learning, choosing, and deciding what is and isn't true.

That's why, beginning with Eve in the garden, Satan has sought to deceive us—to get us to believe his lies. And that's why Paul warned us that we don't wrestle against "flesh and blood" but against principalities and powers (see Eph. 6:12). It's why Peter exhorted us to prepare our minds for action (see 1 Peter 1:13) and to be on the alert (see 1 Peter 5:8).

The seemingly simple choice of what we set our minds on throughout the day can determine the outcome of our spiritual warfare. Just a small deviation from God's standard can put us at risk and lead us far afield from our desired destination. What we choose to read, watch, and think about will largely determine whether we'll be victims or victors, conquered or conquerors.

As a child, I learned the following:

Sow a Thought, and you reap an Act;
Sow an Act, and you reap a Habit;
Sow a Habit, and you reap a Character;
Sow a Character, and you reap a Destiny.[4]

Satan's first step in the battle for our minds is to distract us (see James 1:14-15). The distraction itself may not be sin. In fact, the most effective distractions are those that aren't. It may be something that seems small and insignificant. However, whatever distracts us or weakens our resolve puts us at risk.

What kinds of things distract you? In which areas of your life do you consistently struggle? Are there any particular sins to which you're routinely vulnerable? Are there any activities that consume too much of your time? Over the past years, what has been the most effective "bait" that Satan has used to attract you?

Failure in the area of our moral life is rarely the result of a blowout. Almost always, it's the result of a slow leak. Extramarital affairs, for example, are rarely the product of conscious premeditation. If people were brought to trial for having affairs, few would be found guilty of adultery in the first degree. There are two key factors that can make a person ripe for an affair: emotional vulnerability and an opportunity.

What usually happens is that vulnerable men and women gradually slip into a relationship with someone they feel comfortable with, someone who makes them feel good, someone who "understands them." The infatuation leads to dependence, and they discover that they're deeply involved and it's difficult to disentangle themselves.

If you choose to stay behind the 40-yard-line, and if you guard your heart and mind, you'll be well on your way to becoming "more than a conqueror" (Rom. 8:37). In the Book of Proverbs, we're told, "I would have you learn this great fact: that a life of doing right is the wisest life there is. If you live that kind of life, you'll not limp or stumble as you run. Carry out My instructions; don't forget them, for they will lead you to real living" (Prov. 4:11-13, TLB).

Key 6: Guide Your Eyes

At the beginning of this chapter, I mentioned the struggle I've had with pornography. God has given me significant victory over this area of my life. But it can still happen when I'm walking through an airport bookstore or when I'm at the video rental store looking for a family video. When I see the title of a movie or the seductive picture on the cover, I'm amazed at how sometimes my mind can wander to visualizing what might be inside.

Once it's in that mode, my mind can easily rationalize looking at things that my heart clearly tells me are wrong. They may not be sin, but if they weaken my commitment to sexual purity, they make me vulnerable to even greater temptations, which will lead to sin.

The good news is that as always, with the temptation God provides a way of escape (see 1 Cor. 10:13). After many (too many) years of practice, I've found that I need to go beyond guarding my heart to guiding my eyes. When my internal alarm goes off, I've disciplined myself to look the other way and keep walking. I've learned that if I don't allow my eyes to look at it, it's harder for my mind to dwell on it.

What things should we avoid? Anything our hearts tell us is wrong. For men, it might be something as seemingly innocuous as the Victoria's Secret catalog or the *Sports Illustrated* swimsuit issue.

Hundreds of women have assured me that this principle applies to them too. It isn't just a male issue. If you're a woman, the temptation may come as it did to Sharon, in the form of soap operas or romance novels that stimulate the imagination, fuel an unhealthy fantasy life, increase your dissatisfaction with your husband, and subtly encourage you to look outside your marriage for the love you've been told you "need and deserve."

In Genesis 39, we see that Joseph was smart enough to know you can't play with fire and not get burned. When he was tempted, he ran. He was in such a hurry that he didn't even get his coat or make arrangements with Mrs. Potiphar to retrieve it.

Job knew the importance of guarding his eyes. He wrote, "I made a covenant with my eyes" (Job 31:1). But David followed in the tragic legacy of men who linger too long, stare a bit too much, and unwisely entertain unhealthy fantasy. He didn't guard his eyes and ended up committing adultery with Bathsheba and murdering her husband.

If you want to control a fire, don't pour gasoline on it. Addictive lust is fueled by rationalization and denial. When lust takes control, God seems far away. It doesn't matter what you've experienced, what you believe, or what you know to be true. The little Sunday School song my kids sing has some powerful wisdom for us:

Oh be careful little eyes what you see;
Oh be careful little ears what you hear;

Oh be careful little lips what you speak;
There's a Father up above, looking down in tender love;
Oh be careful little eyes what you see.

Conclusion

Are we facing a moral crisis? Yes! Is it a major problem? There's no question about it! Can one person solve it? Of course not! But can God use us to make a meaningful contribution to the solution? Most definitely! Remember the words of Jesus in Matthew 5:16: "Let your light shine before men, that they may see your good deeds and praise your Father in heaven."

Christ also said, "Whoever can be trusted with very little can also be trusted with much" (Luke 16:10). As a young man, I didn't understand why that was so important. Now I know that in the process of becoming a godly man, there are no little things. In fact, it's how we handle the seemingly small things that over time determines our response to the big ones.

I referred earlier to C.S. Lewis' *The Screwtape Letters.* In one conversation between the senior tempter and his protégé, the experienced demon described the effectiveness of small distractions in defeating Christians:

> But do remember, the only thing that matters is the extent to which you separate the man from the Enemy. It does not matter how small the sins are provided that their cumulative effect is to edge the man away from the Light and out into the Nothing. Murder is no better than cards if cards can do the trick. Indeed, the safest road to Hell is the gradual one — the gentle slope, soft underfoot, without sudden turnings, without milestones, without signposts.[5]

If you allow one thought or activity in your life that you know to be contrary to the clear teaching of God's Word or that your spirit tells you is not best for you, even though it may not in itself be sinful, you'll find that your spiritual eyes will become darkened, your spiritual ears hard of hearing, and your soul numb to the "soft promptings" of the Spirit.

Beware of the temptation to justify or rationalize. Many of my own failures started by moving in a direction my head rationalized by saying, "It isn't sin," but my heart said, "Don't do it." Be on guard for statements such as, "It's not that bad," "I've seen worse," or "The Bible doesn't have anything to say about that." Don't ask what's *wrong* with a certain behavior or choice; ask what's *right* with it. Is what you're considering more likely to move you closer to or further away from your goal of being who God would have you to be?

If there's to be any hope for our marriages, families, cities, nation, and civilization, we must return to and passionately embrace the biblical standard for who God would have us to be. It's not enough to give mental assent to truth or to dance with the truth. We must make a commitment to be men and women who aren't afraid to count the cost and stand tall, at times seemingly alone, but in truth with thousands of other believers who want to make their lives count. Remember that "Blessed — happy, enviably fortunate, and spiritually prosperous — are the pure in heart, for they shall see God" (Matt. 5:8, AMP).

I wouldn't blame you for saying, "Dr. Oliver, that sounds too simple. How can God use little changes in me to affect my family?" But while the impact may not be immediate, it will be long lasting. I promise that the long-term reality of your authenticity will expose the emptiness of the world's pseudo-morality.

Finally, remember that we don't think and act in a void. When we come to the point of temptation, how we respond will depend largely on what we've been doing in the preceding twenty-four hours. That's one reason I faithfully try to keep my morning appointment with God, lifting my thoughts and desires to Him and filling my consciousness with His perspective. It's why I keep watch on my mind and heart and eyes as I move through my day. And I can't recommend strongly enough that you likewise commit your ways to Him and allow Him to direct your paths. "In all your ways acknowledge Him, and He will make your paths straight" (Prov. 3:6).

Small Beginnings

For more than twenty years, I've worked with many individuals who had allowed themselves to become involved in immorality. As they've expressed their pain, grief, guilt, humiliation, and shame, almost all of them have said, "If I had only known what this relationship would cost me and those around me, I *never* would have become involved."

The list that follows are just some of the consequences of moral failure. Read it over, think about it, and the next time you're tempted even a little by immorality, go back and review it.

- Grieving the Lord who redeemed me, and dragging His sacred name into the mud.
- Inflicting untold hurt on my spouse, my loyal best friend.
- Losing my spouse's respect and trust.
- Hurting my beloved children.
- Destroying my example and credibility with my children and nullifying both present and future efforts to teach them to obey God. ("Why listen to a person who betrayed Dad/Mom and us?")
- Bringing shame to my family. ("Why isn't Dad/Mom a Christian leader anymore?")
- If my blindness should continue or my spouse be unable to forgive, perhaps losing him/her and my children forever.
- Losing self-respect.
- Creating a depth and breadth of guilt difficult to overcome. Even though God forgives us, it can be hard to forgive ourselves.
- Forming memories and flashbacks that could plague future intimacy with my spouse.
- Wasting years of academic training and ministry experience for a long time, maybe permanently.

- Undermining the faithful example and hard work of other Christians in our community.
- Bringing great pleasure to Satan, the enemy of God and all that is good.
- Heaping judgment and endless difficulty on the other person if I commit adultery.
- Possibly bearing the physical consequences of such diseases as gonorrhea, syphilis, clamydia, herpes, and AIDS; perhaps infecting my spouse or, in the case of AIDS, even causing his/her death.
- Possibly causing pregnancy, with the personal and financial implications, including a lifelong reminder of my sin.
- Following in the footsteps of these people whose immorality forfeited their ministries and caused me to shudder: (list names)
- Bringing shame and hurt to these coworkers: (list names)
- Causing shame and hurt to these friends, especially those I have led to Christ and discipled: (list names)
- Invoking shame and lifelong embarrassment upon me.

10. Road to Maturity

Since the beginning of time, mankind has been focused on the struggle between winning and losing. In the fourth chapter of Genesis, we read that Cain's desire to be viewed as a winner led to a jealousy that resulted in his murdering his brother, Abel. Many years later, when David was praised for his victory over Goliath, Saul became jealous and attempted to kill him.

In the time of Christ, Roman soldiers were challenged by the battle cry, "To the victor go the spoils!" In the twentieth century, little has changed. The late Vince Lombardi, former coach of the Green Bay Packers, updated that cry by saying, "Winning isn't everything. It's the only thing."

The United States may be the most success-oriented country in the world. People are identified as winners or losers. Our obsession with success and winning cuts across all categories. Neither age, gender, color, education, occupation, religion, nor socioeconomic level seems to matter.

Before winning the Super Bowl in 1998, the Denver Broncos football team had been in the "big game" four times and had lost every one. How do you think the sports media characterized them, as winners or losers? How about teams like the

Minnesota Vikings or the Buffalo Bills, who also lost all their Super Bowl games?

The winning-is-everything philosophy comes at a high cost. When winning is everything, when failure is feared second only to death, we become more vulnerable to the temptation to deceive, distort, compromise, and cheat. When the end result is all that matters, it's easier to rationalize our dishonesty as "not that big a deal" or with the ever-popular "everybody does it."

At the point of victory, those who have triumphed are called winners. And most people don't care how you won the game, got the money, or came in first. You won, and that makes you a winner. However, one of life's painful realities is that often those who appear to win in the short run end up, over the long haul, as losers. Those who win aren't always winners, and those who lose aren't always losers.

When we lose, we can become so devastated by the experience that we also lose our perspective. It's hard to remain objective or rational about ourselves and our failure. It's easy to move from "I failed!" to "I'm a failure, a loser, and I'll never succeed. I've always been a loser, and I'll always be one."

Some people are willing to pay an unbelievable price for their definition of success. Jimmy Johnson provides a classic illustration. When Jerry Jones bought the Dallas Cowboys football team, he shocked the sports world by firing the legendary Tom Landry as coach and hiring Johnson, who had absolutely no professional coaching experience. However, Johnson had been very successful at the college level and was determined to be a success in the pros.

He was so determined, in fact, that he divorced his wife, Linda Kay. He told her there wasn't room in his life for both her and the Cowboys. After suffering through a dismal initial season, he led the Cowboys to two consecutive Super Bowl championships. He was a success. But his wife and kids paid an enormous price.

In an interview with *Sport* magazine, Johnson said, "I don't think there were any mistakes raising my kids." He continued,

"Maybe there were things I'd have done differently, but they weren't mistakes. That's parenting." Then he said, "I almost treated them [his sons] like players—very regimented. That's when I was there. I was gone most of the time."[1]

If you talked to his son Brent, he would say that was true. He told the story of coming home late one night. His dad met him at the door and demanded to know where he had been. Brent had had enough. He said to his dad, "No, the question is, where have you been?" He recalled, "It just bothered me that he would be gone all the time, and then he'd come back to town and lay down all these rules. I didn't think he was in a position to tell me what I can and can't do. So when he asked me where I'd been, I threw it back in his face."[2]

Our obsession with success and the stigma that has been placed on failure pervade every aspect of our lives, including marriage, family, and work. I agree with the nineteenth-century American statesman Charles Francis Adams, who said, "Failure seems to be regarded as the one unpardonable crime, success as the all-redeeming virtue."

In the same vein, Jerry Croghan wrote, "In our society today, the notion that someone is a 'failure' is more powerful and more damning than almost any other label one can apply. People are not ashamed to admit they are materialistic, greedy, alcoholic, sexually deviant, lazy, and so on, but they recoil at the notion that they may have failed at something."[3]

After more than forty-five years of living, studying God's Word, and working with the lives of men and women He has created, I've seen that the fear of failure can become the fatal factor in our ability to live life to its fullest, to become all that God would have us to be. Perhaps no one has said it better than Howard Hendricks: "Failure is one of the uglies of life. We deny it, run away from it, or, upon being overtaken, fall into permanent paralyzing fear."[4] Like an adolescent with zits, we try to cover up our failures. Hide them. Pretend they don't exist. But just like the teenager, sometimes our attempts at hiding things only make them look worse.

You might be surprised at the extraordinary lengths some people will go to in an attempt to appear more successful than they really are. I'm talking about bright people and spiritual people who will go to ridiculous extremes to fool themselves and others. Recently I came across a classic illustration of this. In a fax summary of news and commentary from the *New York Times*, I read that Stanford University's faculty had just voted overwhelmingly to tighten a promiscuous grading system under which hardly any student flunked a class and nearly everyone received A's and B's almost as a matter of entitlement. I was astonished that an academic institution with the reputation of Stanford had deteriorated to the point where they had that kind of grading standard.

The article went on to say that the failing grade would be restored, and teachers would be encouraged to award C's and D's when deserved. It seems that those two letters had virtually disappeared from the dazzling but misleading transcripts that a generation of Stanford students (and those at plenty of other places) had used to impress parents, employers, and graduate-school deans.

"The sad truth is that Stanford's permissive practices were merely the final expression of a sensibility that *seeks to eliminate the fear of failure, holds that feeling good is more important than doing well and assumes that somehow students can be injected with self-esteem rather than earning it by honest toil*" (emphasis mine).[5]

Stanford's practice was tragic on several levels. First, the deception involved damaged the credibility and integrity of one of our nation's most-respected universities. But the biggest injustice was suffered by the students. Because they were encouraged to operate in a mistake-proof system, they were robbed of the opportunity to learn from their mistakes. Even worse, they were taught to accept a false basis for their worth and a false sense of their ability.

In their helpful book *When Smart People Fail*, Carole Hyatt and Linda Gottlieb noted that society's definition of success has four main characteristics:

1. It involves visible accomplishment, actively *doing* something . . . as opposed to *being* something.
2. You must do it yourself.
3. Its rewards are generally in the form of money. If life is a game then money is the way many people keep score.
4. The judgment of success is determined by others.[6]

Unfortunately, this definition of success is not just held by the world. Many Christians have been seduced into accepting a less than biblical view of success and failure. I've heard some Christians teach that our value is based on what we accomplish or what we abstain from rather than an understanding of who God has declared us to be in Christ and who He would have us to become through the process of sanctification. They equate making mistakes with being carnal and immature.

Why are we all so vulnerable to this cult of success? How did we get sucked into the silliness of the "pseudosuccess syndrome"? Most of the reasons can be summarized in one small word—*fear*. Fear is one of the most powerful motivators known to mankind. The fear of failure can be paralyzing and often involves a myriad of other fears: the fear of "not being picked," of being average, of the humiliation of defeat, of rejection, of being labeled a "loser," or of being exposed for who we really are.

For some people, the fear of failure is so great that they spend much of their lives sitting on the sidelines, playing it safe. Rather than getting in the game and risking defeat, they withdraw from activities they might enjoy, activities that God has called them to. Rather than trusting in God and being faith focused, they feed their fears and become failure focused. The more we feed our fears, the fatter they grow and the harder it is to escape them.

So what's the problem? Some would say it's that we've deified success and made it a god. But I don't think that's it. After all, the Bible is clear that God wants us to be successful. He wants us to be more than conquerors. The problem is that we've deified a definition of success that takes man's view as the measure rather than God's. And whenever you measure yourself with a crooked ruler, you'll never get things straight.

God's View of Success

As we saw in chapter 4, God doesn't define success as the absence of failure. He doesn't measure our value in terms of our accomplishments but in terms of the development of Christlike qualities. He looks at success as a direction more than a destination. And He knows that an absolutely essential part of maturing involves stepping out in faith and risking failure.

Paul warned the Christians in Rome, "Don't let the world around you squeeze you into its own mold, but let God remake you so that your whole attitude of mind is changed. Thus you will prove in practice that the plan of God is good, acceptable to Him and perfect" (Rom. 12:2, PH).

We would much rather be identified with those who are high and healthy than with those who are lowly and hurt. We want to be numbered with the climbers and comers, not the lepers and losers. The temptation to become conformed to this world (and this world's recipe for success) is as seductive as it is strong.[7]

When the world defines success, it starts with the creation. We need to start with the Creator. To understand God's view of success, we need to know Him and understand His plan for our lives. J.I. Packer began chapter 3 of his best-selling classic, *Knowing God*, with the following dialogue:

What were we made for? To know God. What aim should we set ourselves in life? To know God. What is the "eternal life" that Jesus gives? Knowledge of God. "This is life eternal, that they might know thee, the only true God, and Jesus Christ, whom thou hast sent" (John 17:3).

What is the best thing in life, bringing more joy, delight, and contentment, than anything else? Knowledge of God.

"Thus saith the Lord, Let not the wise man glory in his wisdom, neither let the mighty man glory in his might, let not the rich man glory in his riches; but let him that glorieth glory in this, that he understandeth and knoweth me" (Jeremiah 9:23ff).

What, of all the states God ever sees man in, gives Him most pleasure? Knowledge of Himself. "I desire . . . the knowledge of God more than burnt offerings," says God (Hos. 6:6).[8]

God's Word is clear. The experience of hundreds of thousands of men and women who have gone before us is clear. The starting place for a happy, abundant, and successful life is in knowing God through an intimate, personal, and growing love relationship with Jesus Christ.

Referring again to John 17:3, notice that Jesus didn't say eternal life is knowing *about* God. There are many sources of information about God. Over the years, I've discovered that a person can accumulate vast stores of knowledge about God and still not know Him or become like Him. I've had teachers who could exegete the Greek text of 1 Corinthians 13 with brilliance but in whom there was little visible costly love. In my own life, there have been times when I've taught about how to overcome temptation and then turned around and fallen for the most elementary trick in Satan's book.

Ephesians is one of the most glorious books in the New Testament. If you ever find yourself wading through the muck and mire of discouragement, pick up your Bible and read those six short chapters. They'll change your perspective and renew your spirit. At the end of the third chapter, Paul brought the first section to a close with a moving prayer for the Ephesian believers. In verse 19, he asked God to bring them to the place where they could "know the love of Christ which surpasses knowledge, that you may be filled up to all the fullness of God."

What a great request! What a wonderful experience! And it

gets better. In the next verse, he described God as the One who is able to do "exceeding abundantly beyond all that we ask or think" (NASB). As we learn what it means to "know" the love of Christ that "surpasses knowledge," we'll be filled with the fullness of God and experience Him who is able to do far more than we could ever ask or imagine. Is that exciting or what?

Several years ago, I heard a wonderful illustration of the difference between the head knowledge of the Pharisees in Jesus' day and the heart knowledge Paul wanted for us. A wealthy family had invited one of the world's most famous orators to their home for a reception. Out of courtesy, they had also invited their pastor.

At the end of the reception, someone in the crowd asked the gifted speaker to recite something. "What would you like to hear?" he asked.

The crowd was silent. They couldn't think of anything. Finally the elderly pastor said in a squeaky voice, "I would love to hear you recite the Twenty-third Psalm. It has always been my favorite."

The orator agreed, but only on the condition that after he gave his rendition, the pastor would come to the front and give his. The pastor reluctantly agreed. The guest stood tall, took a deep breath, and began, "The Lord is my shepherd, I shall not want." When he came to the end of the psalm, the group applauded.

Then the pastor slowly made his way forward. Because he wasn't very tall, when he finally got to the front, some of those in the back couldn't see him. He stood there for a moment, then in his frail voice began, "The Lord is my shepherd, I shall not want." When he was finished, the crowd didn't clap, but several people had tears in their eyes.

The renowned orator came over to the pastor and put his hand on his shoulder. He turned to the crowd and said, "Tonight the reverend gave you a far better rendition of this psalm than I did." After a brief pause, he continued, "It's obvious that while I know the Twenty-third Psalm, *he knows the shepherd.*"

That's the difference between head knowledge and heart knowledge. Head knowledge helps us memorize the psalm, know who wrote it, and identify what kind of psalm it is. Heart knowledge comes from walking with and knowing the voice of the Shepherd.

Throughout the Bible, we find that God takes the initiative to reveal Himself to His people by personal experience. That's why the Bible has so much to say about loving God. Love isn't just a casual intellectual commitment. God's plan for us is a relationship with Him, not a job description.

You'll never be satisfied or successful if you only know *about* God. Truly knowing Him only comes through experience as you walk with Him, talk with Him, and allow Him to reveal Himself to you, especially in the midst of your failures.

In Acts 4:13, we see that as the people noticed the changed lives of Peter and John, they remembered that they had been with Jesus. Romans 8:29 tells us that God's desire for us is that we "become conformed to the image of His Son" (NASB). In 2 Corinthians 3:18, Paul wrote that we're "being transformed into the same image" of Christ. Head knowledge can give us valuable information. But only heart knowledge leads to transformation. And transformation involves growth.

In 1 Corinthians, Paul expressed concern over the Corinthian Christians because they hadn't grown: "And I, brethren, could not speak to you as to spiritual men, but as to men of flesh, as to babes in Christ" (1 Cor. 3:1, NASB). The writer of Hebrews expressed concern that his readers hadn't deepened or matured (see Heb. 5:11-14). He started chapter 6 by exhorting them to "press on to maturity" (6:1, NASB). He was really saying, "Hey, folks, it's time for you to make some changes. It's time for you to grow up."

A willingness to change, learn, and grow is God's love language. It says we believe in Him, trust Him, and want to be who and what He wants us to be. It's our way of taking His hand and following where we don't always understand, where we fear, because of our faith in Him.

In 1 Peter 1, Peter used a powerful word picture to describe the growth process. He compared our lives to gold that's purified by fire. The refining process involves several different firings in which the heat brings the alloys and impurities to the surface of the molten gold so the goldsmith can remove them. The refining process takes time and hard work, but the product is worth it. The end result is pure gold.

God uses many things to fuel the fire in the refining process of our lives. One of the most powerful and at times most frustrating involves our failures. God can use them to produce the heat that brings our weaknesses and impurities to the surface. He can use the light of our failure to see our flaws, and beyond our flaws to opportunities for growth.

In fact, it can be through the disappointment, discouragement, and frustrations of failure that we learn to see through the eyes of Christ and gain the mind, the love, the patience, and the forgiveness of Christ. Each time the gold of our lives is reheated, different alloys and impurities are brought to the surface. At each step of the process, the gold is a bit different from what it was before.

I would go so far as to suggest that God's definition of success can best be summarized in the word *growth*. As we mature, as we manifest the fruit of the Spirit, we're becoming successful. Look at the following list of synonyms for the word *grow:*

become	expand	develop	enlarge
blossom	augment	supplement	extend
mature	advance	bud	shoot up
progress	thrive	bear fruit	bloom
prosper	flourish	luxuriate	

I remember hearing Warren Wiersbe say in a radio message, "We can benefit from change. Anyone who has ever really lived knows there is no life without growth. When we stop growing, we stop living and start existing. But there is no growth without change, there is no challenge without change. Life is a series of changes that create challenges, and if we are going to make it, we have to grow."

At the beginning of this chapter, I told the story of Jimmy Johnson and his view of success. In contrast to that, we have the example of another professional athlete. Tim Burke loves the game of baseball as much as Jimmy Johnson loves football. From the time he can first remember, his dream was to be a major league baseball player. Through years of sacrifice and hard work, he achieved that goal.

While he was a successful pitcher for the Montreal Expos, he and his wife wanted to start a family, but they discovered they weren't able to have children. After much prayer and soul searching, they decided to adopt. Eventually they became the parents of five special-needs international children.

What followed was to be one of the most difficult decisions of Burke's life. He discovered that his life on the road conflicted with his ability to be a quality husband and dad. Eventually it became clear that he couldn't care for his family adequately and still play baseball. After more prayer and soul searching, he made what many considered an unbelievable decision. He decided to give up professional baseball.

When he left the stadium for the last time, reporters wanted to know why he was retiring. "Baseball is going to do just fine without me," he said. "It's not going to miss a beat. But I'm the only father my children have. I'm the only husband my wife has. And they need me a lot more than baseball does."[9]

Burke acknowledged that "many people have a hard time understanding how I could walk away from all the acclaim and the money that are such a part of major league baseball. . . . All my life I dreamed of being a major league pitcher. For eight wonderful seasons, I fulfilled that dream. Now I have a bigger dream. I want to be a major-league husband and a major-league dad."[10]

When all is said and done, a biblical view of success involves the following five characteristics:

1. It involves pursuing excellence in becoming conformed to Christ.
2. It's a process. It takes time, and it involves stepping out in faith and learning from our failures.
3. We can't do it by ourselves. We need the indwelling presence of the Holy Spirit, the Bible, and the church.
4. Its rewards are both temporal and eternal. Sometimes it involves money. Often it involves things that money can't buy and that time can't erase.
5. The judgment of success is determined by God and validated by His Word and the testimony of faithful Christian friends.

All of us want to be winners. But the ways in which we define success and failure will determine the degree to which we ultimately win or lose. Every day we make choices. Jimmy Johnson made his choice. Tim Burke made his. Which one of those men is a success, and which is a failure?

God wants us to become like our Lord Jesus Christ. But growth involves change, doing something different, and that moves us out of our comfort zone. Yet what's the result of choosing to play it safe, of choosing not to grow? I hope you agree with Chuck Swindoll when he said:

It is vital — it is essential — that we see ourselves as we really are in the light of God's written Word . . . then be open to change where change is needed. I warn you, the number one enemy of change is the hard-core, self-satisfied sin nature within you. Like a spoiled child, it has been gratified and indulged for years, so it will not give up without a violent temper tantrum. Change is its greatest threat, and a confrontation between the two is inevitable. Change must be allowed to face and conquer the intimidations of inward habit — and I repeat the warning that a nose-to-nose meeting will never be an easy one.

The flesh dies a slow, bitter, bloody death — kicking and

struggling all the way down. "Putting off" the clothes of the old man (the old, habitual lifestyle) will not be complete until you are determined to "put on" the garment of the new man (the new, fresh, Christian lifestyle). The tailor's name is Change, and he is a master at fitting your frame. But the process will be painful . . . and costly.[11]

When we understand God's recipe for success and the vital role failure plays in the process, it becomes much easier for us to take the risks that can result in growth. It's a long-term project. It will be painful at times. But going through it with Him sure beats any alternative.

Small Beginnings

1. How would you have defined success before you started reading this book? How would you define it now?
2. What are three ways in which the world's view of success and God's differ?
3. In light of what you've just read in this chapter, what's one specific thing that God might have you do to "go on to maturity"? (Heb. 6:1)

11. Helping a Friend Who Has Failed

As I sit down to write this final chapter, I'm reminded of one of my all-time favorite movies, *The Wizard of Oz*. Do you remember the scene where Dorothy has her second meeting with the grand wizard? She has defeated the evil and wicked witch of the east. She has successfully led her three friends through great peril to meet the wonderful, all-powerful, and all-wise wizard. They have great expectations of what he'll be able to do for them. He's strong. He's wise. He's their hero. He can do anything. They're counting on him.

Then little Toto pulls back the curtain, and the *real* wizard is exposed. He's a short, overweight, and not-too-impressive specimen of masculinity. And, even worse, he's a fraud. With a mixture of anger and despair, Dorothy cries out, "You are a terrible man!"

With a sad but understanding look on his face, he replies, "No, I'm not a terrible man. I'm just a terrible wizard."

When our friends are in crisis, many of us feel like the wizard. We're not terrible people. But we are human and imperfect. We don't always know what to do. We're not sure what to say. We're not necessarily as confident and secure as we appear, and sometimes we're afraid of saying or doing the wrong thing.

What should I say? What shouldn't I say? Those are some of the questions I asked myself when a friend from church called and, after the usual pleasantries, told me that he had been fired from his job after being employed for only five months. That was bad enough. But what made it worse was that Ed had been fired from his previous job as well and had struggled through a year of unemployment before he received the "answer to prayer" of his new job—the one he had just been fired from.

With a pain in his voice that couldn't be fully expressed in words, he said, "Gary, I feel like giving up. It seemed as if things were finally starting to turn around. And now this." After a long sigh, he added, "I haven't told Judy or the kids yet. I don't know how to tell them." And after one more pause, "I don't know if I *can* tell them."

I had supported Ed through the loss of his first job, the roller-coaster ride of the unemployment, and the joy of finally landing a new job. I had walked with him through what I thought was his lowest point. But now I heard a new depth of discouragement and despair in his voice.

One of the first things I did was to check whether his depression was leading him to consider suicide. He told me it wasn't, yet I was still concerned. Ed was overwhelmed by the fact that "I'm a failure. A loser. Any man who can't keep a job and support his family isn't really much of a man."

The shock of the loss, the meaning of the loss, and the potential humiliation of exposure threw him into an emotional meat grinder. Before he walked into his manager's office, he had felt on top of the world. When he walked out, he felt shocked, confused, discouraged, drained, and depressed.

The overwhelming rush of emotions that can hit us during a time of crisis leads to a massive loss of perspective. Ed was so problem focused that there was no way he could have heard anything that might have sounded like a solution. He hadn't just failed. He saw himself as a failure. There's a big difference between the two. The first one merely *describes* a part of you. The second one *defines* you.

As we continued our conversation, I listened to what he had to say. I could tell him he was still a person of value. Or I could show him by making the time to listen patiently to him. As with most people who suffer setbacks, Ed started off asking the terminal "Why did this happen to me?" and then continued on the endless quest for the illusive cause.

Why is it so hard to help a friend who has failed? There are many different reasons. The most powerful is that most of us aren't sure what to do. Another is that it gets us in touch with some of our own past pain. It can also tap into our own fear of failure.

So what do we do at a time like that? What do we say? What don't we say? What does the friend need? Are we able to help? These are important questions that, if you haven't been faced with them already, someday you will be.

I knew what Ed didn't need was someone who had taken the same counseling course as the three guys who counseled Job. He didn't need someone to shame, blame, assume the worst, offer simplistic solutions, or stick his face into what had happened. He didn't need someone to tell him, "Grow up! Take it like a man. You're not the first man who has been fired. Where's your faith? Just trust God."

When you're faced with a friend in need, remember the three words that are essential at railroad crossings: stop, look, and listen. The first step is to stop. Choose to take some time out of your busy schedule to give to your friend. When Ed called, I was in the middle of something that had to get done. But the still, small voice of the Holy Spirit told me I could afford an hour for my friend.

As you stop, remember that at the outset, hurting people need comfort, encouragement, and perspective. They can't see the forest for the "trees" of their problems. The pain of the temporal is blinding them to the perspective of the eternal. The question isn't how do they *deserve* to be treated? It's how do they *need* to be treated?

As Gordon MacDonald observed:

Both inside and outside the church are broken-world people, and they are there in no small numbers. They yearn
for an understanding and wise ear; they dearly wish for an
amnesty that would provide the chance to make things
right and new. If their spirit is right, they are not asking
that their sins be diminished or overlooked; they are not
asking that people pretend nothing has happened. What
they seek is what the cross of Christ offered: grace freely
given; healing fully applied; usefulness restored.[1]

Without grace and the gift of time, broken hearts and shattered dreams take much longer to heal. When someone you love
fails, remember how Jesus responded to Peter: He gave him
acceptance but not approval, understanding and not condemnation, and honesty rather than condescension.

Have you ever thought about how a healthy family and
friends support each other during times of failure? Have you
ever seen parents at a football game when their son is playing?
Imagine that their son is a quarterback and he just threw an
interception. Would they be yelling, "Take the bum out! Toss
the clown! He's a loser!" Or would they be saying, "That's
okay, son! Don't lose your concentration! You can do it, son!
Take them back down the field!"

The first thing about the way a healthy family responds is
that the family members are there. They show up. They let him
know they're with him, alongside him, and behind him. If
you've ever been blindsided by a major failure, perhaps you
know the power of just having someone who cares enough to
be there and "check in" with you.

Second, a healthy family knows the value of encouragement.
They know the incredible power of being a Barnabas. For a
moment, imagine that you're the one who threw the interception. You look up in the stands, and your parents aren't even
there. What might you feel? Or they are there, but they're hiding
their heads. What might you feel now? Or they are there, but
they're shouting criticisms. What would you feel now?

Now imagine that you look up in the stands and see their faces. You still see that proud gleam in your mom's eyes. You can tell from the look on your dad's face that he's with you. You can just make out their words of hope, encouragement, and support. Now what are you feeling?

There's no simple, foolproof way to help a friend who has failed. There's no magic phrase you can use or verse you can quote that will heal the hurting heart or close the open wound. But by God's grace, there are some things you can do to help wipe away some of the tears so they can see a bit more clearly. And you don't have to be a pastor or a trained counselor. Anybody can stop. Anyone can choose to be there and to be available to be used of God.

Once you've stopped, the next step is to look. First look around at what God has been doing in your own life. What has He taught you in recent months? Are there any passages of Scripture that have been especially helpful to you? Has He given you a song that has ministered grace to you in a special way? He may have already been preparing you for this time. Take a good look. You probably have resources you aren't even aware of.

Then look up to God in prayer. Ask Him for power, perspective, patience, and wisdom. Remember what James said: "If any of you lacks wisdom, he should ask God, who gives generously to all without finding fault, and it will be given to him." That's a powerful verse. But don't stop yet; go on to the next: "But when he asks, he must believe and not doubt, because he who doubts is like a wave of the sea, blown and tossed by the wind" (James 1:5-6).

The third simple step is to listen. When confronted with someone in need, as soon as you think *What should I say?* remember this wise one-word answer: *Nothing!* Start by looking, listening, and *then* talking. When it comes to helping someone, we often get the formula backward. We tend to talk and talk and then maybe look and listen.

I've made that mistake for much of my life. When I would

think about comforting a friend, I would focus on talking. But when a hurting friend is speaking, it's important to develop the habit of listening attentively to what he or she has to say. Notice I said *develop the habit.* It's not easy to be a good listener.

You can show your love and concern for a friend through good eye contact, smiling, nodding, and allowing the person to talk uninterrupted. Sometimes he or she will have more to say than you have the time, at the moment, to listen to. In my first conversation with Ed, it felt as if a verbal dam had burst and he could have gone on all night. I didn't have all night. However, I was able to communicate my concern and willingness to take some time. I also encouraged him to call one of our friends who had recently been through a similar situation. At the end of our conversation, I set a time to get together with him.

After you've stopped and spent ample time looking and listening, it's time to talk. But when you do talk, don't start by giving advice. Start by asking questions. A question says, "I've been listening to you. I'm with you. In spite of what has happened, you're still valuable. You're worth taking the time to understand better. Your hurt and pain are important to me. *You* are important to me."

There are two kinds of questions: closed-ended and open-ended. A closed-ended question is one that can be answered with a yes or no, such as, "Do you feel hopeless?" An open-ended question requires more than a one-word response, such as, "How can I be most helpful during this time?" It's usually better to ask open-ended questions.

When asking a question, be sure to give the person enough time to respond. If you push for a response too quickly, it can apply pressure and send the wrong message. While you intended to communicate "You are important," the message received can be "What you have to say is important as long as you can say it quickly. I have a lot of other things to do."

Be sure to give the person permission to express emotions. So often when someone is in crisis, we want to fix it quick. In the process, either through our own discomfort or the awkwardness of the individual's pain, we try to sew up a wound that hasn't been cleaned out.

Remember, emotions aren't always rational. And emotional responses aren't always rational. But they're still valid. Sometimes there isn't a logical reason for what a friend is thinking or feeling.

Through lack of education or misinformation, many people have been educated out of knowing when they're feeling something or what they're feeling. When they were depressed, they were told it was only discouragement. When they were sad, they were told to cheer up. When they were angry, they were told to keep their cool. When they felt pain, they were told to be brave and smile. But part of what it means to be made in God's image is that we have emotions. Birds fly, fish swim, and people feel. To deal with the wide range of emotions that can occur during a difficult time, we have to be able to identify and communicate them. We aren't always free to chose the emotions we'll experience. But with God's help, we can learn how to understand and express them.

Early in the healing process, it's much more important for people to know *what* they're feeling than it is to know *why* they feel it. When they know what their feelings are, they're less likely to feel all mixed up inside.

In further conversations with Ed, I had the opportunity to describe some of the pain I had experienced in my own valleys, and how God had used that pain in my life. I explained some of the ways in which God had helped me to recognize the roots of my own failure. At this stage, the goal is to be open and honest, perhaps to the point of exposing our own sinfulness or stupidity.

In Luke 22:32, Jesus told Peter, "When once you have turned again, strengthen your brothers" (NASB). Others can learn from our experiences of failure. God has designed us to live interdependently. We need to be transparent so that we can minister to others. If all our failures are kept as personal secrets, the body of Christ suffers. While we don't want to wear our experiences on our sleeves, we can become involved with people in meaningful ways so that they experience us as being genuine.

When a friend fails, don't just stand there and stare at him — jump in with him, identify with him, risk being transparent with him, and be more concerned with what God thinks than with what people might say!

In a subsequent conversation, Ed looked at me and said, "I had absolutely no idea of the struggles you've had with depression." His response surprised me since I had revealed some of my own "stuff" in our group. He continued, "That really makes it easier for me to apply truth to my own life." Somehow, as I gave him the opportunity to look into my own imperfect life, he had a kind of model for what God was trying to help him implement in his own.

As I noted back in chapter 3, when people are in the midst of failure, they have a distorted view of maturity and success as a *lack* of struggle rather than involving the *process* of struggle. I reminded Ed that we're all in process. In 2 Corinthians 3:18, Paul observed, "We . . . are being transformed." He used the Greek word for *metamorphosis,* becoming something completely new. Our willingness to embrace the truth about our failures affects our capacity for change. If we refuse the truth, we block the Holy Spirit's renewing of our lives.

Martin Luther said it well,

> This life is not a being holy but a becoming holy; it is not a being well but a getting well; it is not a being but a becoming; it is not inactivity but practice. As yet we are not what we ought to be, but we are getting there; the task is not as yet accomplished and completed, but it is in progress and pursuit. The end has not been reached, but we are on the way that leads to it; as yet everything does not glow and sparkle, but everything is purifying itself.[2]

Stop! Look! Listen! These are three simple steps that anyone can do. Even you. As your friend or loved one gets his or her bearings, you'll want to introduce the person to the twelve steps of growing through failure. You may want to walk through the first several steps with the individual. (See chapters 5 and 6 for all the details.)

With a lot of courage, determination, patience, and support, Ed made it. It took some time. But several months after we'd had our first conversation, I received a note from him. It was so encouraging and well-written that I kept it. With his permission, I've reprinted part of it below:

Dear Gary,

When you first told me that God could meet me in my failure, my first thought was, "Obviously this guy doesn't have a clue about how deep my fear and pain is." Well, I was wrong.

The problem wasn't that you didn't understand my pain. It was that I didn't fully understand God's love for me, the power of the body of Christ, and how to apply the specific truths of His Word to this seemingly impossible situation in my life. I didn't understand the process involved in becoming more mature.

As you risked sharing some of your failures, the shame of doing something you knew was wrong, the humiliation of letting people down, it helped me gain a little perspective. I saw that I wasn't the only one. I began to be able to understand the enormous difference between failing and being a failure.

Your prayers were a comfort. The verses you shared, although they probably seemed to fall on deaf ears, gave me my first taste of hope. I'll never see Psalm 40:1-3, Matthew 6:33, Romans 8:28-29a, 1 Corinthians 10:14, or the fourth chapter of Philippians in the same light again. I remember thinking "It can't be that easy." This time I was right. It wasn't easy, but it was simple. It was just a matter of being faithful, keeping at it, and not giving up.

I still have down days. But not as many as I used to, and they don't last as long as they used to. The bulk of my life is characterized by healthy focus on looking for God's hand in this painful but already productive process.

When I was a young Christian, I memorized 1 Peter 5:7, "Casting all your anxiety upon Him, because He cares for you." Now I can say that I not only know that verse in my head, but I am proving it in my heart and life and marriage.

There's no such thing as a painless life. There is only walking through the inevitable pain with the courage and perspective that come from a personal relationship with the living God. As you choose to allow Him to use you in helping a friend face the pain of failure, you'll find new strength and courage.

In John 20, we find that the disciples' fear kept them locked in a room, hiding under the beds. But when their perspective became renewed, when they realized Jesus had, indeed, risen from the dead and was alive, they became fearless. They moved out in power and conviction, even willing to face a painful death for their Lord.

In Paul's second letter to Timothy, we find that the apostle had left Timothy in Ephesus as the leader of the church there. His job was to combat heretics, order the church's worship, select and train its elders, regularize the relief ministry to its widows, and teach the Christian faith. He was a young man, probably in his early thirties, and had been given a lot of responsibility and authority. He was prone to illness and was fairly timid in nature. Apparently Timothy was a bit overwhelmed by it all and had some apprehensions. But Paul reminded Timothy of his heritage and his call, and then he said, "For God has not given us a spirit of timidity, but of power and love and discipline" (2 Tim. 1:7, NASB).

Today you may have family, friends, or coworkers who feel they're in the rising waters of failure. They may be clinging to whatever they can find, perhaps not knowing where to turn, hoping someone will come along and help them out. I pray that

God will use the tools and insights you've read in this book to expand your vision for how God can use you, increase your courage to take the risk of reaching out, and be willing to take the time to stop, look, and listen — and then speak the wonderful words of life to that friend who's in need.

Finally, remember that failure is never the end but a growing experience, that the God who made you loves you, and that nothing can ever separate you from His love.

Notes

Chapter 1

1. John Lord with Jeffrey Wold, *Song of the Phoenix* (Stockbridge, Mass.: Berkshire House, 1992), p. 26.
2. Quoted in *Psychology of Losing*, p. 161.
3. Words and music by William J. Gaither. © 1963 William J. Gaither. ASCAP. All rights reserved.
4. Source unknown.
5. Quoted in Robert T. Lewis, *Taking Chances* (Boston: Houghton Mifflin Co., 1979), p. 4.
6. Cited in *National Geographic*, December 1978, pp. 858–82.
7. Arthur Gordon, "On the Far Side of Failure," *Reader's Digest*, September 1961, pp. 22–24.

Chapter 2

1. Radio broadcast.
2. Dietrich Bonhoeffer, *Psalms: The Prayer Book of the Bible*, no. 3 (Minneapolis: Augsburg, 1970), pp. 64–65. Used by permission of Augsburg/Fortress.
3. Gordon MacDonald, *Rebuilding Your Broken World* (Nashville: Oliver-Nelson, 1988), p. 30.
4. Source unknown.
5. David Swartz, *Dancing with Broken Bones* (Colorado Springs, Colo.: NavPress, 1987), p. 59.
6. From "CATHY" cartoon by Cathy Guisewite. Used with permission of Universal Press Syndicate.
7. John Lord with Jeffrey Wold, M.D., *Song of the Phoenix*, p. 110.
8. Richard Dortch, *Integrity: How I Lost It and My Journey Back* (Green Forest, Ark.: New Leaf, 1993), n.p.

Chapter 3

1. MacDonald, *Rebuilding Your Broken World*, pp. 164–65.
2. Harold Kushner, *When Bad Things Happen to Good People* (New York: Avon, 1981), p. 3.
3. Carole Hyatt and Linda Gottlieb, *When Smart People Fail* (New York: Simon & Schuster, 1987), p. 19.
4. Words by Gloria Gaither. Music by William J. Gaither. © 1971 William J. Gaither. ASCAP. All rights reserved.
5. David D. Burns, *Feeling Good* (New York: Morrow, 1980), p. 21.

6. D. Martyn Lloyd-Jones, *Spiritual Depression: Its Causes and Cure* (Grand Rapids, Mich.: Eerdmans, 1966), pp. 10–11.

7. Dorothy L. Sayers in *Dorothy L. Sayers: Spiritual Writings*, cited in *Christianity Today*, March 1994, p. 42.

8. MacDonald, pp. 38–39.

9. Quoted in MacDonald, *Rebuilding Your Broken World*, pp. 28–29.

10. Ibid., p. 29.

Chapter 4

1. Erwin Lutzer, *Failure: The Back Door to Success* (Chicago: Moody, 1975), p. 51.

2. Max Lucado, *No Wonder They Call Him the Savior* (Portland, Ore.: Multnomah, 1986), pp. 93–95.

3. Quoted in Paul Brand and Philip Yancey, *Pain: The Gift Nobody Wants* (New York: HarperCollins, 1993), p. 300.

4. Adapted from Philip H. Mirvis and David N. Berg, eds., *Failures in Organization Development and Change* (New York: Wiley, 1977), p. 3.

5. Vic Sussman, "To Win, First You Must Lose," *U.S. News & World Report*, Jan. 15, 1990, pp. 64–65.

Chapter 5

1. C.S. Lewis, *The Screwtape Letters* (New York: Macmillan, 1961), p. 47.

2. Ibid.

3. Jack Hayford, *Men of Action*, Fall 1994, p. 7.

4. Words and music by Brown Bannister and Mike Hudson, © 1978 by Bug and Bear Music and Home Sweet Home Music.

5. Jeffrey T. Jernigan, "Failure: One of Life's Best Teachers," *Decision*, September 1993, pp. 27–29. © 1992 Billy Graham Evangelistic Association. Used by permission. All rights reserved.

6. Oswald Chambers, *My Utmost for His Highest* (Aug. 26), edited by James Reimann, © 1992 by Oswald Chambers Publications Assn. Ltd. Original edition © 1935 by Dodd Mead & Co., renewed in 1963 by Oswald Chambers Publications Assn. Ltd. Used by permission of Discovery House Publishers, Box 3566, Grand Rapids, MI 49501. All rights reserved.

Chapter 6

1. MacDonald, *Rebuilding Your Broken World*, pp. 67–71.

2. John Gardner, *Self-Renewal*, in MacDonald, p. 74.

3. Oswald Chambers, *The Place of Help*, emphasis mine, in *Rebuilding Your Broken World*, p. 50.

4. Eugene H. Peterson, *A Long Obedience in the Same Direction* (Downers Grove, Ill.: InterVarsity, 1980), p. 25. Used by permission of InterVarsity Press, P.O. Box 1400, Downers Grove, IL 60515.

5. MacDonald, p. 157.

6. Haddon W. Robinson, "Call Us Irresponsible," *Christianity Today*, April 4, 1994, p. 15.

7. Adapted from John Holt, *Why Children Fail* (New York: Pitman, 1964), p. 34.

Chapter 7

1. Michael J. O'Neill, "Let's Hear It for Losers!" *Newsweek*, Nov. 2, 1987, p. 9.

2. Adapted from Wallace Terry, "When His Sound Was Silenced," *Parade Magazine*, December 25, 1994, pp. 12–13.

3. Eugene Peterson, *The Message* (Colorado Springs, Colo.: NavPress, 1993), p. 21.

4. Quoted in Richard J. Foster and James Bryan Smith, eds., *Devotional Classics* (San Francisco: HarperSanFrancisco, 1993), pp. 192–93.

5. Richard J. Foster, *Prayer: Finding the Heart's True Home* (San Francisco: HarperSanFrancisco, 1992), pp. 1–2.

6. Nancy Spiegelberg, *Decision*, November 1974, n.p.

7. Gordon MacDonald, *Restoring Your Spiritual Passion* (Nashville: Oliver-Nelson, 1986), p. 105.

8. Traci Mullins, "Defeating the Fear of Failure," *Discipleship Journal*, No. 36, 1986, p. 7.

9. Adapted from the following articles: David A. Kaplan, "The Best Happy Ending," *Newsweek*, February 28, 1994, pp. 44–45; Paul A. Witteman, "Finally," *Time*, February 28, 1994, n.p.; Alexander Wolff, "Whooosh!" *Sports Illustrated*, February 28, 1994, pp. 19–23.

10. Miles J. Stanford, The Green Letters (Lincoln, Neb.: Back to the Bible, 1991), p. 27.

11. Quoted in The Green Letters, pp. 15–16.

12. Foster, *Prayer*, p. 71.

Chapter 8

1. Source unknown.

2. Norman Vincent Peale, *Dynamic Imaging* (Old Tappan, N.J.: Revell, a division of Baker Book House, 1982), pp. 186–187.

3. David Radavich, "In Life, What's Important Is That You Lose," *U.S. News & World Report*, August 24, 1987, p. 5.

4. Earl Gustkey, "Former Trojans Endure Anguish at Tampa Bay," *Los Angeles Times*, November 4, 1977.

5. "Losing Made Us More Determined," Hertel, Orange Coast (Calif.) *Daily Pilot*, quoted in *Taking Chances*, p. 174.

Chapter 9
1. By P.P. Bliss in Alfred B. Smith, *Inspiring Hymns* (Grand Rapids, Mich.: Zondervan/Singspiration), 1951, p. 456.
2. Quoted in *Devotional Classics*, p. 185.
3. Quoted in William J. Bennett, *The Book of Virtues* (New York: Simon & Schuster, 1993), p. 461.
4. Quoted by Samuel Smiles in *Bartlett's Familiar Quotations*, 13th ed., p. 1005.
5. C.S. Lewis, *The Screwtape Letters*, pp. 64–65.

Chapter 10
1. Steve Buckley, "The Happiest Man in America?" *Sport*, July 1993, pp. 26, 28.
2. Ibid., p. 28.
3. Jerry Croghan, "The Psychology of Art," *American Artist*, August 1988, pp. 18–21.
4. Quoted in Erwin Lutzer, *Failure: The Back Door to Success*, p. 9.
5. "The Value of Failing," *TimesFax*, June 5, 1994, p. 8.
6. Hyatt and Gottlieb, *When Smart People Fail*, p. 31.
7. Adapted from Cornelius Plantinga, Jr., "Assurances of the Heart," *Christianity Today*, June 20, 1994, n.p.
8. J.I. Packer, *Knowing God* (Downers Grove, Ill.: InterVarsity, 1973), p. 29. Used by permission of InterVarsity Press, P.O. Box 1400, Downers Grove, IL 60515.
9. Tim and Christine Burke with Gregg Lewis, *Major League Dad* (Colorado Springs, Colo.: Focus on the Family, 1994), p. 5.
10. Ibid., pp. 241, 247.
11. Charles R. Swindoll, *Come Before Winter . . . and Share My Hope* (Portland, Ore.: Multnomah, 1985), pp. 331–32.

Chapter 11
1. Gordon MacDonald, *Rebuilding Your Broken World*, p. 222.
2. Quoted in Ewald M. Plass, compiler, *What Luther Says, Vol. 1* (St. Louis: Concordia, 1959), p. 235.